baby
sign language
made easy

BABY SIGN LANGUAGE
made easy

101 SIGNS TO START COMMUNICATING
WITH YOUR CHILD NOW

lane rebelo

ILLUSTRATIONS BY BORIS STOILOV

ROCKRIDGE
PRESS

For general information on our other products and services or to obtain technical support, please contact our Customer Care Department within the United States at (866) 744-2665, or outside the United States at (510) 253-0500.

Rockridge Press publishes its books in a variety of electronic and print formats. Some content that appears in print may not be available in electronic books, and vice versa.

Illustrations © Boris Stoilov, 2018

Photography © Oksana Kuzmina/Shutterstock.com, cover; Jacquelyn Warner, author photo; leungchopan/iStock.com, p. ii; Lane Rebelo, p. v; onebluelight/iStock.com, p. vi; Melpomenem/iStock.com, p. xii; santypan/iStock.com, p. xvi; FatCamera/iStock.com, p. 12; simarik/iStock.com, p. 40; Ridofranz/iStock.com, p. 54; Sasiistock/iStock.com, p. 68; sam74100/iStock.com, p. 80; PeopleImages/iStock.com, p. 102; monkeybusinessimages/iStock.com, p. 122; SolisImages/iStock.com, p. 140; LPETTET/iStock.com, p. 141–142; ulimi/iStock.com; 13goat/iStock.com; SergeiKorolko/iStock.com.

ISBN: Print 978-1-64152-077-5 | eBook 978-1-64152-078-2

R1

Printed in Canada

To Clara and Annie, my original Tiny Signers.
I love you to the moon and back.

contents

2. The First 10 Signs 13

3. Mealtime and Manners 41

6. Playtime and Out and About 81

7. Animals 103

8. Family and Feelings   123

introduction

WELCOME TO *Baby Sign Language Made Easy!* You hold in your hands the book I wish someone had handed to me when I decided to try signing with my first baby.

When I became a mom back in 2006, I was curious about baby signing and borrowed a book from the library to learn more about it. The book gave me a lot of information about the history and theory of using basic sign language with hearing babies, as well as instructions for a lot of signs, but it didn't tell me *how* to introduce signs to my baby. It also didn't offer much in the way of tips or strategies for success.

Despite the shortcomings of that book, I did go on to have success signing with my first daughter, Clara. I began with hopes that she'd learn a few signs to let me know when she was hungry or if she wanted something, but the experience turned out to be much more than I ever imagined. Signing opened a window into her mind and allowed me to understand what she was thinking through the signs she used. I was blown away by the ability to see the world through her eyes, and to this day I feel that signing deeply and forever shaped our connection because we were able to communicate so early on. That's not to say we didn't hit a few stumbling blocks along the way. In fact, for days, I didn't notice her first sign because it didn't look like what I expected, and I didn't know what to look for! To make sure this doesn't happen to you, I've included tips on what baby's early signs may look like so you know what to look out for.

I quickly got hooked on signing and learned all I could about it, training with experts and researchers in the field and taking American Sign Language (ASL) classes at a local school for the Deaf. In 2009, I created Tiny Signs®, and since then I've been teaching classes and workshops to parents, educators, and early childhood professionals. I've had the privilege of working with so many wonderful families over the years, and I continue to learn from them every day as they bring me new and unique questions. I never grow tired of hearing the exciting news that a little one has made her first sign or of helping my students trouble-shoot challenges. Signing is such a powerful tool, and its impact on families continues to amaze me, even after all these years.

When my second daughter, Annie, was born, it was a given that I'd sign with her, as well. What I didn't anticipate was how all the skills I had acquired from teaching would impact my experience with baby number two. She started signing back to me on the very day we started! By her first birthday, she knew nearly 100 signs and was also combining signs into two-word sentences (for example, **MORE CRACKERS**).

I wrote this book to share the signs, tips, and tricks that have helped me and so many other families find success with baby sign language. That said, your baby doesn't need to learn 101 signs to make a huge impact on both of your lives. Even just a few key signs can transform your early interactions. I've included illustrated instructions for 101 signs, so you can pick and choose based on your baby's age, ability, and interests.

My wish for you is that you'll find this book to be a quick and simple guide that shows you just how fun and easy it is to integrate sign language into your everyday routine with your baby. I want you to discover the wonder of early communication and see for yourself just how smart your little one is!

HOW TO USE THIS BOOK

This book is geared toward new parents, expectant parents, grandparents, caregivers, nannies, educators, and child care workers. It's meant for just about anyone who spends time with infants and toddlers and wants to learn how to communicate with them before speech develops.

As a busy (and usually sleep-deprived) mom myself, I know you don't have the time or desire to read hundreds of pages about the history of baby sign language, a summary of all the research ever done on the topic, or 1,001 activities you can do with your baby. I get it. This book gives you the exact information you need to get started, plus tips and realistic strategies for success, delivered in an easy-to-understand format.

Throughout the book, you'll find 101 of the most commonly used, practical signs to teach your baby. There are literally thousands of signs you could learn, but to help you get started, I've focused on the ones that have been most successful with the families I've taught as well as in my personal experience as a mom. The 101 signs in this book should keep you going for quite some time, but if you want to expand your vocabulary beyond the scope of this book, or learn more about ASL, I've included resources to help you continue in the Resources section.

The beginning of the book covers the basics. Chapter 1 includes a quick overview of baby sign language as well as answers to common questions. Chapter 2 presents the first 10 signs to learn and provides tools and tips to start using them right away. These first signs are indispensable for babies. If you're working with an older child, however, or if your baby is already signing, you can jump right to the subject matter that interests your child.

The remaining chapters are organized by theme in order of usefulness and include mealtime, getting dressed, bath time and bedtime, playtime, animals, family, and feelings. Once your baby has started signing, you'll want to continue to expand her signing vocabulary, and these chapters are chock-full of great options.

You might have purchased this book with the practical goal of teaching your little one a handful of signs to reduce frustration and make your day-to-day life a little easier. This book will definitely help you reach that goal! I do hope you'll keep an open mind to the possibility that signing can offer so much more than just functional communication (which alone is remarkable). If you continue to grow your signing vocabulary beyond the basics, I know you'll be blown away by what your little one understands and observes in the world. You'll have so much fun as your baby uses signs to tell you about the dog he saw outside or how much he loves blowing bubbles with you. You have the opportunity now to get to know your baby's interests and personality a year or more earlier than you would have if you waited until he started talking. Take advantage of this exciting opportunity and be prepared to be amazed!

1

Baby Signing Basics and FAQ

IN THIS CHAPTER, I will walk you through the basics of baby sign language to help you feel confident and informed as you get started. You'll learn about signing at different ages and developmental milestones as well as answers to the questions I most commonly hear from people new to baby sign language. My goal is to give you enough information for you to feel knowledgeable on the topic but not overwhelmed with a ton of information and research. You're reading this book, so you already know that signing with babies is a fantastic way to start communicating before they're able to talk. So let's get right to the good stuff!

WHAT IS BABY SIGN LANGUAGE?

Here's how I define *baby sign language*:

> The practice of pairing American Sign Language (ASL) vocabulary with spoken words to facilitate early communication with preverbal, hearing babies.

All babies communicate through gestures, whether you teach them sign language or not. All babies learn to wave and point, and they will often lift their arms to signal when they'd like to be picked up. Babies do this because their gross and fine motor skills (the ability to move their arms and hands) develop earlier than their speech. Babies naturally bridge this gap by using their ability to gesture to express themselves. Baby sign language builds on this very natural ability to make it even more useful. I promise it's easy. Trust me, if an 8-month-old can do it, so can you!

In the above definition, you might have noticed I specified American Sign Language, or ASL. In this book, all the signs you'll learn are ASL. Using made-up gestures or simplified versions of ASL signs for babies can cause confusion, as caregivers and books might contradict each other. Sticking to ASL keeps things consistent and helps avoid confusion about how to do signs. You'll just be acquiring basic ASL vocabulary, or signs, which is a lot

easier than trying to become fluent in ASL. Learning fundamental ASL signs for communicating with your baby is like picking up very basic words of another spoken language. I think of it as *Dora the Explorer*-level learning. You'll learn how to sign **DOG** (page 31), **WATER** (page 49), and **TREE** (page 90), but not how to string signs together into complete sentences.

ASL is an incredible language used by the Deaf community in the United States and most of Canada. There are many ASL websites, books, DVDs, and classes out there if you want to learn more. I've included information about some of these in the Resources section at the back of this book.

WHEN TO START TEACHING

The first question I usually get about baby sign language is, "When is the best time to start signing with my baby?"

The short answer is that you can start any time. However, it's important to have realistic expectations.

Signing is no different from other developmental milestones such as sitting up, crawling, and walking. All babies are different and have their own timeline. Below are some general guidelines for what to expect, but remember that every child develops at her own pace.

- *Some* babies might make their first sign as early as 5 months old

- *Most* babies start signing back in the 8- to 12-month range
- *Some* babies might make their first sign after their first birthday

So start signing now, but if your baby is under 6 months, keep in mind that it might be some time before you see that first sign. But don't give up! All babies will sign back if you stick with it and follow the advice in the pages ahead.

MAKE TEACHING FUN

Teaching signs to baby should be enjoyable for both you and your little one, which is why I've included the Signing Fun section at the end of each chapter throughout the book. This is another teaching tool, offering easy songs, books, and activities to do with your baby to practice signs. You'll find classic children's songs and books with sign illustrations on the same page so you can sign key words while reading or singing. And most of these activities don't require any additional materials—just a sense of humor and a willingness to try something new!

You also might find it helpful to see the signs you've learned in this book in action. I've created a **free video dictionary** of all the signs in this book on my Tiny Signs® website (TinySigns.net/book-owner), where you can find short videos of me demonstrating each of the signs.

DEVELOPMENTAL MILESTONES

As you begin signing and communicating with your little one, it might be helpful to know what to expect developmentally. The following information will give you an idea of some typical milestones for both speech and signing. Of course, keep in mind that all babies are different, so these milestones should be used only as a general guideline. If you have any concerns about speech and language development, be sure to mention it at your baby's next checkup with your pediatrician.

infant development at a glance

0 TO 6 MONTHS OLD

- Baby's vision is still developing, so it's important to sign within one to two feet away
- Baby's memory is still developing
- Motor abilities are emerging, like holding head up, rolling over, and sitting with support
- Baby is working on gaining control of her hands and arms
- Baby might recognize and respond to your signs before being able to sign back
- Benefits of starting to sign in this age range include making signing a habit and building vocabulary
- Keep realistic expectations—most babies won't begin to sign until 8 months

6 TO 12 MONTHS OLD

- Period of rapid gross motor development begins (scooching, crawling, pulling up, taking first steps)
- Baby starts sitting independently, freeing hands and arms to use for signing
- Baby begins actively exploring her world
- Most babies start signing in the latter half of this age range

12+ MONTHS OLD

- Baby learns to walk, can stand on her own, and crawls up stairs
- Baby's receptive language (what she understands) is highly developed
- Speech is beginning to develop and first words appear
- Gap between understanding of language and ability to communicate usually causes frustration for baby and caregivers
- Babies learn signing very quickly at this stage!

speech versus signing milestones

0 TO 6 MONTHS OLD

Speech:
- Coos
- Gurgles
- Babbles
- Responds to your voice

Signing:
- May recognize and respond to your signs
- Babbles and plays with hands
- Might make first sign

6 TO 12 MONTHS OLD

Speech:
- Has increased range of vocalizations
- Mimics sounds

Signing:
- Recognizes your signs
- May make 1 to 10 (or more!) signs

12 TO 18 MONTHS OLD

Speech:
- May say first words (*mama, dada, baba*)
- Might communicate interest by pointing
- Understands majority of key words in familiar context (*dog, cracker*)
- Can follow simple one-step directions ("Touch your tummy!")

Signing:
- May make 1 to 50 (or more!) signs
- May begin combining signs into simple sentences (**MORE WATER**)

18 TO 24 MONTHS OLD

Speech:
- May say 1 to 20+ words
- Jabbers incoherently at times
- Follows simple one- and two-step instructions

Signing:

- May make 100+ signs
- Combines spoken words with signs
- May combine signs into simple sentences

24+ MONTHS OLD

Speech:

- May say 50 to 100+ words
- Says simple sentences ("Daddy bye-bye")
- Parents and caregivers might not be able to clearly understand child's speech at this stage

Signing:

- Combines spoken words and signs to communicate
- Uses signs to clarify spoken words
- May begin dropping signs as speech replaces frequently used signs

FREQUENTLY ASKED QUESTIONS

Here are answers to the questions I am most often asked about signing with babies.

Are learning and teaching baby sign language hard?

Definitely not! To start, all you need to learn are a few ASL signs. Then you can add more and keep learning right along with your baby. ASL signs are easy to learn because they often look similar to the items they represent. Just look at

page 34 to see how much the ASL sign for **BOOK** looks just like a book! I also provide a tip for remembering each sign right alongside the signing instructions to make it even simpler.

As far as teaching baby sign language, you really don't have to do anything special. I don't recommend scheduling special time to "teach" your baby sign language. That's totally unnecessary and might even backfire if your baby feels pressured to learn. Just add signs to your regular routines and playful interactions. Chapter 2 includes lots of strategies for getting your baby's attention and making signing fun. You'll also find great songs, books, and activities throughout the book, which are fun and easy opportunities to sign with your little one.

Can I start signing with a newborn?

If you have a newborn baby, or are expecting, and you are eager to start signing, should you wait? Not necessarily.

Some babies start signing as young as 5 months old, so you never know—your little one might surprise you. Just keep in mind that it's not typical for babies to start signing this young, so you might be signing for quite a few months before you are celebrating that first sign back. But it will happen if you stick with it!

It's important to remember that your baby will recognize and respond to your signs well before he ever makes his first sign. Even before your infant is signing back, it is still beneficial to sign to him early on and set the groundwork

CONTINUED ON PAGE 7

how baby sign language can help with speech delays and other special needs

There are a number of developmental issues that can greatly impact a child's ability to communicate, including Down syndrome, autism spectrum disorder, and apraxia. These challenges can affect a child's ability to speak clearly or even speak at all. Sign language can be a lifesaver for families faced with the challenge of trying to communicate with a child who is unable to express his needs and wishes verbally.

Often, developmental issues are not discovered until a child is out of the baby stage, leaving parents wondering if they've missed the chance to take advantage of the benefits of baby sign language. The answer to that is, emphatically, no. Baby sign language can be used with *any* child, regardless of age, who is unable to form words or communicate via speech.

In terms of methods, teaching a child with special needs to sign is really no differ-ent from teaching an infant or toddler to sign. Follow the guidelines outlined in this book for choosing the signs to start with as well as the techniques in chapter 2 on how to introduce signs to your child.

If you're teaching a child with special needs to sign, adjust your expectations for how long it might take that child to start signing based on his unique skills and abilities. Model the signs you'd like the child to learn frequently and consistently. Slow the signs down and speak clearly so the child has ample opportunity to see and hear the word. If the child doesn't object, gently guide his hands to show him how to do the sign himself. Be patient and encouraging.

When looking for a child to sign back, keep in mind that his version of the sign might be limited by his motor skills and range of motion, depending on his abilities. Keep your eyes open for any movement that appears to be purposeful and repetitive, and compare it to the signs you have been using in order to identify what the sign might be. Celebrate your amazing child's ability to communicate with you using sign language, and pat yourself on the back for providing him with a tool to connect with the world around him.

for using your hands (along with your voice) to communicate. If you start using signs as part of your daily routines early on, you yourself will benefit by establishing strong habits, and signing will become second nature.

One last important thing to keep in mind when signing with your baby at this early stage: Your baby's vision is still developing during these early months, so he's focused on things within about a foot or so of him. That means that if you're signing from across the room, he's not going to see you. Any signing done during these early months needs to be in pretty close proximity to your baby.

Which signs should I start with?

I've made this super easy for you. In chapter 2, "The First 10 Signs," you'll find the signs I recommend starting with—these are based on my 10 years of experience teaching all kinds of families and children baby sign language. They represent the most *useful* signs and the best *playful* signs to start with as well as invaluable tips for how to start teaching a baby to sign. It's my tried-and-true method that always leads to success!

The useful signs include **MILK** (page 25), **EAT** (page 26), **MORE** (page 27), **ALL DONE** (page 28), and **BED** (page 29). They represent what you as a parent or caregiver will likely most want to know: What does my baby want and need right now? Is she hungry? Is she tired?

The playful signs include **DOG** (page 31), **LIGHT** (page 32), **BALL** (page 33), **BOOK** (page 34), and **CAR** (page 35). Playful signs represent what your baby is interested in and wants to talk to you about. (Yes, your baby wants to talk to you about her interests!) I include the playful signs because in my experience, they are often the key to getting a baby to start signing.

If a baby already knows a few signs and you know you want to start with food signs or feelings, then go ahead and jump to the chapter that covers the signs you're looking for, but I still recommend reading chapter 2 for all the tips and strategies you'll find there.

When will my baby be able to sign back?

That really depends on your baby's age and individual development. As mentioned in Speech versus Signing Milestones (page 4), most babies start signing in the 8- to 12-month range, so if your little one is under 6 months old, it could be a few months until you see that first sign. If your baby is in the 6- to 12-month range, it could take a few weeks to a few months. If your baby is over 12 months, it could be a few days to a few weeks. Basically, the younger your baby is, the longer it will be until you see that much-anticipated first sign. But don't let that discourage you! I promise it will be worth the wait. And the practical suggestions you'll find throughout this book will set you up for success.

Is it too late to start teaching my toddler sign language?

By the time babies reach 12 months, their receptive language (what they understand) has really exploded! They understand almost everything said to them, even though they may be speaking only one or two simple words. This is the time when sign language really becomes an essential tool for communication.

If you have a toddler (generally considered to be between 12 and 36 months old) and haven't started signing yet, you may be wondering if it's too late. The first year of your baby's life can go by in a blur. You might not have even thought about signing until you found yourself with a frustrated toddler on your hands. Not to worry! It's definitely not too late to start, and the good news is, your little one will likely pick up signing really quickly at this point.

We all know that tantrums can become a real issue during this stage of development. Most tantrums stem from frustration around not being able to communicate—that's where signing can really help. You'll find that your toddler has a *lot* to say, and giving her the tools to express her thoughts and wishes will alleviate meltdowns.

So what are you waiting for? Jump in and start learning some signs for your toddler's favorite foods, toys, and activities. You'll see your child's frustration decrease and everyone's happiness increase.

Aren't ASL signs too hard for babies to do?

Some ASL signs, like **DOG** (page 31) and **HAT** (page 61), are pretty easy for babies to do, while others, like **BUTTERFLY** (page 92) and **SISTER** (page 128), are more complicated for little fingers. However, the same can be said for spoken language. Words like *mama* and *dada* are much easier for new talkers to say than words like *elephant* and *spaghetti*. Does that mean we shouldn't use big words with babies? Of course not! Babies understand complex words just fine, and when they are able, they will make their best effort to say them (often leading to some adorable mistakes!). When a baby's best attempt to say *elephant* comes out sounding more like "fafayent," we simply cheer him on and continue to model the correct pronunciation. "That's right, sweetie, that is an *elephant*—look at its long trunk!"

Signing is no different. Your little one will do his best to mimic the ASL signs you introduce. Some of his signs will hit the mark pretty closely, while others might leave you scratching your head. We call these early attempts at signing and speaking "approximations," which is a fancy way of saying the baby is giving his best effort. Just like with spoken language, there's no need to simplify ASL for babies—just know that their early attempts may look quite different from how you do it, and that's just fine. Continue modeling the sign the correct way, and encourage the baby's effort. You don't need to fix or correct those signs (in fact, doing so might discourage your baby from signing), so just make a note of his version and continue modeling the correct way. In time, as your baby's skills develop, his signs will evolve to look more like yours. To help you recognize approximations, I've included some clues for what a baby's version of each sign may look like.

Will signing delay my baby's speech?

In a word, no. Numerous studies have been done on this topic, and if anything, research has shown that signing with babies has a positive impact on their language development. While there have been many studies done on this topic, the most influential research began in the 1980s by researchers at University of California. In one of their many studies, the researchers compared a group of infants who were exposed to signs and gestures with a control group of infants who were exposed only to speech and found that signing actually improved verbal language development overall. So you can be confident that signing will not hamper your baby's speech—it will likely help it!

Does everyone need to sign to the baby?

In an ideal world, everyone would do things just the way you do. But we all know that's not how things work. So while it would be great if your partner, the baby's grandparents, and the babysitter all signed with the baby, it's okay if they don't. It's still a good idea, however, to get others on board as much as possible. Once you've started signing with your baby, you can let others who spend time with her know which signs you are using and show them how to do them. If they're not interested in learning something new, that's okay—just carry on signing with your baby when you're spending time together. You can still succeed in signing on your own.

Sometimes people who were reluctant to try signing at first will come around once a baby starts signing back and they see for themselves just how amazing and helpful it is. Once the baby does start signing, it's important to communicate to all caregivers what the signs look like and what they mean. As mentioned before, a baby's early versions of signs might not look perfect, so you'll need to let others know what to look for. For example, if you've taught your baby the sign for **MORE** (page 27), and her version of **MORE** looks like touching her pointer finger to her open palm, let her other caregivers know that when she does that motion, she wants "more." You can even write it down as a reference for caregivers to keep handy. Even a caregiver who might not have been interested in teaching the baby to sign at the beginning should want to know how to understand her signs once she starts communicating. It will make everyone's life easier!

Fortunately, signing has become more and more common in daycare settings, so hopefully you won't run into any problems there. Feel free to give this book to the other caregivers in your baby's life to help answer any questions or concerns they might have about signing with your little one.

How do we sign in a bilingual household?

I often get asked by families who are using two spoken languages with their baby, "Will signing just make things more confusing?" My answer to this is always a resounding "Absolutely not!" The fact is that signing can actually *help* your baby make the connection between the two spoken languages, accelerating the learning process and facilitating better communication all around.

Here's how it works: As babies' receptive language develops, they begin to associate a spoken word with an object. For example, a baby will learn that the spoken word *cat* means that furry thing that walks around the house. An English/Spanish bilingual baby will need to learn *cat* = that furry thing and *gato* = that furry thing, then also make the connection that *cat* and *gato* have the same meaning.

When you are signing with your bilingual baby, you can make this process much easier. When you say "cat" in English while signing **CAT** (page 105) in ASL, then say "gato" in Spanish while signing **CAT** in ASL, you are showing your baby that they mean the same thing and ultimately speeding up the learning process.

One of my favorite benefits of signing with bilingual babies is it provides an opportunity to know what they understand in both languages. For example, a family who took classes with me shared their amazement when their baby signed **PEACH** (page 43) when her grandparents mentioned the word conversationally in Mandarin. Before that moment, they had no idea just how much of her grandparents' language she was really picking up!

If you are planning to use two spoken languages with your baby and have any concerns that signing might confuse things, please don't worry. Baby sign language is a wonderful tool to enhance communication in your bilingual home!

How do I learn more?

This book includes 101 of the best and most useful ASL signs. In addition, you'll find instructions for how to sign the ASL alphabet and numbers on page 141. While you probably won't be teaching your baby how to fingerspell his ABCs anytime soon, this section will definitely be a handy reference. Why? Because quite a few of the signs in this book use the handshapes from the ASL alphabet. For example, the sign for **WATER** (page 49) is made with a *W* handshape (page 142), and the sign for **PLAY** (page 83) is made with *Y* handshapes (page 142).

If you're like me, you might just fall in love with learning ASL and want to go beyond the 101 signs you'll find in this book. That's great! If this is you, check out the websites in the Resources at the back of this book to learn more about ASL.

② The First 10 Signs

ONE OF THE FIRST decisions you'll need to make as you begin signing is which signs to try first. In this chapter, you'll find my top 10 signs to start with, which are separated into two categories: *useful* signs and *playful* signs. Useful signs are the signs that parents and caregivers typically think of when signing with babies, like **MILK** (page 25) and **EAT** (page 26). Playful signs are important because they work with baby's interests and motivations. Some popular early playful signs are **DOG** (page 31) and **BALL** (page 33).

Choosing the right signs to start with will have a direct impact on how quickly your baby signs back. Most parents come to baby sign language for the promise of improved communication and reduced frustration, and signing definitely delivers on both. However, when first starting out, you'll need to think a little outside the box if you want to fast-track your success. In this chapter you'll also learn how many signs to start with and when to add more.

But most importantly, in this chapter you'll learn *how* to teach the signs to your baby. You'll find my top tips and strategies for success, including how to incorporate signing into your day and how to capture your baby's attention to make signing fun and engaging for both of you.

USEFUL VERSUS PLAYFUL SIGNS

As parents and caregivers, we tend to think of the very practical words we use every day when thinking about signs to start with. The signs you might already have in mind are things like **MOM** (page 125), **MILK** (page 25), **DIAPER** (page 56), and **BED** (page 29). Because feeding, changing, and getting your baby to nap are the things that consume your days lately, am I right? Totally understandable!

I call these kinds of signs *useful signs*. These are the signs that will make life with your baby a whole lot easier because he will be able to tell you when he's hungry, when he's sleepy, or even when he needs a diaper change. Another great thing about useful signs is that you have the opportunity to use them over and over throughout the day at every feeding, changing, and nap. This gives you lots of chances to practice signing to your baby.

Useful signs you'll learn in this chapter are **MILK** (page 25), **EAT** (page 26), **MORE** (page 27), **ALL DONE** (page 28), and **BED** (page 29). You'll find tips on introducing these signs and more in the following pages. The signs about diaper changing, like **DIAPER** (page 56), **CHANGE** (page 56), **POOP** (page 58), **CLEAN** (page 58), and **DIRTY** (page 59), are a bit more advanced, so these will come later in the book and in your sign language journey. And while useful signs are really practical, you might be surprised to learn that they might not be your baby's first signs.

In fact, **the biggest secret to signing success is working with your baby's interests** to fast-track the process. Playful signs are those that will motivate your baby to start signing back, and they are different for every baby. Think about it this way: If you were getting your basic needs met by communicating one way (crying), what would motivate you to communicate another way? The playful signs motivate your baby to form signs so she can "talk" to you—and once she realizes you understand her, she will learn the useful signs, too. Picking the right playful signs boils down to figuring out what tends to capture your baby's attention, which you might already know. Does she kick her legs every time she sees something? Or does she point, or smile, or make noises? If you're not sure, spend a little time today or tomorrow observing your little one. Here are some questions to help get your wheels turning:

Is there something your baby seems mesmerized by? The ceiling **FAN** *(page 85) or* **LIGHT** *(page 32)?*

Look at your home environment. Do you have a large **FISH** *(page 108) tank? Or a pet* **CAT** *(page 105) or* **DOG** *(page 31)?*

Does your baby have a favorite toy? Maybe a chewy **GIRAFFE** *(page 116) or a favorite lovey* **BLANKET** *(page 75)?*

While playful signs will be different for every baby, I have some tried-and-true favorites that are consistent winners, so don't worry if nothing comes to mind right away. I've got you covered. The playful signs you'll learn in this chapter are the ones I've seen reliably work as first signs. They include **DOG** (page 31), **LIGHT** (page 32), **BALL** (page 33), **BOOK** (page 34), and **CAR** (page 35). You'll find instructions on how to do these signs, as well as suggested activities, in the following pages.

HOW TO TEACH SIGNS

Teaching your baby sign language sounds hard, but I promise that it's actually really simple. Baby signing is about building on a baby's natural ability to gesture—to wave, reach, or clap. Have you ever heard anyone talk about how hard it was to teach a baby to wave bye-bye? Of course not! If you wave and say "bye-bye" to a baby enough times, he'll start to mimic you and eventually do it unprompted. Baby sign language works in the exact same way. I've included some tips below to take the intimidation out of the teaching process. Remember, it's supposed to be fun!

choosing signs to start

When first starting out, I recommend starting with **four** signs: two Useful Signs (page 24), and two Playful Signs (page 30). This is a manageable number to learn and use often.

Four well-chosen signs give you good odds that you've picked at least one or two that will spark your baby's interest and get the learning process started. However, if you'd like to start with one or two more, feel free to do so. Just remember that your baby's early signs might not be easy to understand, so if you start with lots and lots of signs and the little one starts doing what you think is an early attempt at signing, it will make it harder to figure out which sign it is.

when to add more signs

After you've been signing regularly with your baby, you might wonder when it's time to add more signs to the routine. There are two good times to add more signs: The first is when you've been at it for a while and feel ready to branch out a bit. Just remember to add to the signs you started with—don't drop any of the ones you're already using! For example, if you started signing when your baby was 3 months old and you've been signing four signs for a few weeks, you may be ready to add some more. The second time to add more signs is once your baby starts signing back. Then it's go time! Once signing "clicks" for your baby, you want to build on the momentum by expanding your signing vocabulary and introducing more signs.

How many signs you add really depends on your comfort level for learning signs yourself and working them into interactions with your baby. You might want to introduce one new sign each week, or you might find yourself adding a new one each day. There's no "right" way, so do what feels right for you.

CONTINUED ON PAGE 18

5 ways to capture baby's attention

One of the challenges of teaching sign language to babies is that they have to be looking at you in order to see the sign. This can be tricky if they are focused on the item you are trying to sign for them. For instance, what if you want to teach the sign for **CAT** (page 105), but every time the cat enters the room, your baby's eyes are glued to the furry object of his affection?

Not to worry! Here are some pro tips on getting your baby to look at you so you can successfully teach new signs.

Bring the item to you

One way to bring your baby's eyes to you is to gently take the item she's focused on and slowly move it toward you so her gaze follows the object. For example, if the baby is holding a ball and you can't get her to look at you, gently take the ball away from her. Put the ball in your lap, sign **BALL** (page 33), and pay attention to where she is looking. If she is looking at the ball in your lap instead of at your hands, move your hands into her line of sight. Or try holding

the ball in your hands and sign **BALL** with one hand. The objective here is not to frustrate or upset your baby, but rather to show her the sign, so be sure to tread lightly and return the object quickly.

Make some noise

Another great way to get a baby's attention is to make interesting sounds. Your baby loves your voice and will look to you when you do something unusual. You can capture his attention by making funny or silly noises. You can bark like a dog or gently gasp as you reveal something you think he would be interested in discovering. Also, if you have something that makes noise, like a jingly set of keys or a toy that squeaks, you can use the noise of the object to get your little one's attention. When he looks at you to see what's going on, seize the opportunity to show him a sign.

Get touchy-feely

You can also sign right on your baby's body. Certain signs, like **DOG** (gently pat baby's thigh; page 31) and **BATH** (gently "scrub" your fist on baby's chest; page 71), are perfect for this technique. This is a great way to introduce signs to a little one in a multi-sensory way.

You can also move your baby's hands to help her do the sign. For example, bring your baby's hands together to show her how to sign **MORE** (page 27). A word of caution, however: Some babies really don't like this (they'll show they don't like it by tensing up and pulling back). If your baby isn't a fan, skip this approach—it's not worth creating a negative association with signing. Also, if you do use this technique, don't fuss over helping your baby do the sign "right." Just move her hands in the general motion of the sign so she gets the idea.

Get up close and personal

It's important to sign in close proximity (within a few feet) to babies during the first year, as their vision is still developing. One of the great things about ASL is that you can move your hands to bring the sign right into your baby's line of sight. Instead of waiting for your baby to look at you, you can simply bring the sign right to him without interrupting his activity. This is a very effective way to introduce a sign. Your baby will simply absorb the signing information along with the other information he is taking in.

Wait for it

Another option for introducing a new sign is simply to wait for your baby to look at you. Babies frequently check in visually with their parents or caregivers to see how they are reacting to any given situation. Babies do this to gauge their own emotional response to their environment. If you get in the habit of signing when your baby looks at you, she will likely check in with you visually even more to see if you are signing. This creates more opportunities to teach new signs!

sign and say the word together

When signing with your little one, always sign and say the word together. Babies learn language by watching and hearing you speak. Saying the word every time you sign it will increase your baby's exposure to spoken language and also provide an opportunity to associate the spoken word with the sign. Throughout this book you'll notice that some words are in **ALL CAPS**. This signifies that the word is meant to be signed while being spoken out loud.

sign in context and repeat key words

As parents and caregivers, we naturally narrate our activities to babies as we move through our routines. You might notice yourself repeating key words as you talk to your baby, for example, "Do you see that *bird*? What a colorful *bird*! Do you see the *bird's* blue feathers? That *bird* is looking for a worm. I bet that *bird* is hungry!" This speech pattern is often referred to as "parentese," which is a melodic and repetitive way of speaking to young children that offers lots of exposure to common words. Adding signs to those key words when speaking is an excellent way for babies to see and learn new signs.

When you are first starting out, you should always sign in context. That means if you are signing **BALL** (page 33), there should be a ball within sight, or if you are signing **CAT** (page 105), the cat should be nearby or visible in the book you are reading. Signing in context will help your baby make the connection between the sign and its meaning.

sign in baby's line of sight

Obviously, it's important for the little one to be able to see what your hands are doing in order to learn to sign. Often when you're talking to your baby, she'll be looking at your face. Sometimes in order for her to see the sign, you might need to modify the sign to get it into her line of sight. For example, the sign for **MORE** (page 27) is signed in front of your torso. However, with a baby, you might want to move your hands up and closer to your face to make the sign easier to see. In order to pick up a new sign, babies need to see it in action.

keep it fun

The most important rule for signing success is to have fun! Approaching signing with a playful attitude will make it a positive experience for both you and the child. For babies, playing *is* learning. If signing feels like a chore to you, it probably will to the baby, too. Keep it light-hearted. Use silly voices and animated faces. Lose your inhibitions and sign like nobody is watching. And if one of you is having an off day, give yourself a break and come back to it tomorrow. He won't be able to learn something new when he's cranky and tired.

TROUBLESHOOTING

It is so exciting when your little one starts signing! Communicating with signs is like opening a magical door into children's minds, allowing you to actually see what they are thinking as they talk to you with their signs.

As wonderful as baby sign language is, however, sometimes there are bumps along the road that can surprise and confuse parents and caregivers. Here are some of the possible scenarios so you'll know what to do if you encounter one.

i'm not sure if my baby is signing

As mentioned previously, the earliest versions of a baby's signs (approximations) can often be tricky to identify. Is he trying to sign **MORE** (page 27)? Or is he just clapping? Sometimes, a baby's signs are easy to miss, or they can be mistaken for something else. If you find yourself wondering if your baby is signing or not, use the guidelines in Recognizing Baby's Signs (page 22) as well as the 👁 *What to look for* tips throughout this book to help identify baby's earliest versions of signs.

baby is using the same sign for everything

Being able to communicate is exciting! You might find that once your baby starts signing, she uses her favorite sign all the time, which can be really confusing! You might find yourself wondering, "Does she really want **MILK** (page 25) *again*?" If this happens to you, take heart and know that this is a phase and it will pass. There's an old saying that goes something like, "If you only have a hammer, everything looks like a nail." By teaching your baby a sign (or two), you've given her an amazing hammer, and she wants to test it out and see what it can do. Using the same sign for everything is also a good indicator that you should teach more signs so she has more tools in her toolbox, so go ahead and add more signs as you feel ready. Refer to When to Add More Signs (page 15) for tips on growing your signing vocabulary.

it feels like my baby is *never* going to sign back

If you've been signing diligently to your baby for weeks (or months) with no response, it can get really discouraging. You might even be tempted to give up. Will he ever sign back? The answer is yes! Refer to Speech versus Signing Milestones (page 4) for a refresher on what to expect. Don't give up! I've had a number of students whose babies hadn't started signing after 12 months, and they were really discouraged. But then their little ones started signing like crazy, and they were amazed at how many signs they knew and how fast they were picking up new ones. Don't give up on signing—it *will* happen if you stick with it, I promise! Also, make sure you're not missing your baby's signs. This happens more often than you'd think. Refer to Recognizing Baby's Signs (page 22) to learn how to look for early signs.

all of my baby's signs look the same

When your baby first starts signing, signs that have similar movements—for example, **MORE** (page 27), **BALL** (page 33), and **SHOES** (page 63)—can look basically the same and be difficult to tell apart. Frustration might creep in because you can't be certain which sign he is doing. I encourage you to step back for a moment and instead be amazed that your baby is trying hard to communicate with you well before he is able to speak—that's incredible! Always remember, the early versions of his signs will evolve and improve. A month or two from now, you might find yourself wistfully thinking, "Remember when he used to sign **BALL** like this?" So, try not to rush the process. And make sure you use the suggestions in Recognizing Baby's Signs (page 22) to help distinguish between early signs.

baby is doing the sign wrong

It's important to keep in mind that your baby's early attempts at signing can look quite different from how you do it, *and that's perfectly fine.* Applaud your little one's best effort and continue modeling the sign the correct way. Resist the temptation to fix or correct her signs. In fact, correcting your baby might actually discourage her from signing. To keep making progress, make a mental note of her version and continue modeling the sign the correct way. In time, as her skills develop, her signing will improve. See Recognizing Baby's Signs on page 22 to learn more about spotting these early signing attempts. You'll also find 👁 *What to look for* tips throughout this book.

baby made up his own sign

Once babies get the hang of signing, they sometimes will make up their own signs for things they are eager to "talk" about. This is an amazing development. Your baby is actively trying to build his vocabulary. When this happens, you have two choices: Teach him the correct sign or stick with the made-up sign. If the sign is for a common word, such as *train* or *cracker*, I would recommend learning the ASL sign and start using it whenever possible to replace the made-up sign. If the made-up sign is for something unique, however, like a particular lovey or a special food you make at home, then you might choose to incorporate the invented gesture into your vocabulary.

baby stopped signing altogether

This speed bump can be especially confounding and frustrating! You've spent weeks or months signing and your baby finally started signing back, but then, for seemingly no reason, she stopped using her regular signs altogether. What happened? Sometimes, when babies are working on another big milestone—like pulling up to stand or taking first steps—they stop signing temporarily to focus all their mental energy on mastering a new skill. Or, if a baby has a cold or is cutting new teeth, she might also take a signing break. If this happens, just keep signing. Know that she *will* resume signing once she's moved through whatever has been consuming her energy and attention. It can be frustrating when this happens, but it usually doesn't last long. Hang in there!

baby is dropping some signs

As babies grow and develop, things can get really interesting. Sometimes a baby that used to sign **MILK** (page 25), **APPLE** (page 42), **CEREAL** (page 44), **YOGURT** (page 44), and **CRACKER** (page 46) starts using the sign

YOGURT for all of these foods, which might feel like a step backward. However, what has actually happened is a developmental leap forward: Your little one has started to sort words and objects into categories. This is an important milestone. If this happens, let your baby know you see how clever he is. You can say something like, "That's right, **YOGURT** is something we **EAT** (page 26)!" However, if you suspect he doesn't actually want yogurt, you can encourage him to pick up dropped signs by saying something like, "Do you really want **YOGURT**, or do you want **PASTA** (page 47)?"

most importantly: stick with it

Your little one will throw some curveballs your way as you start communicating with signs. Try not to get discouraged. Always remember that you and your baby are communicating on a level that wouldn't be possible at all if you weren't using baby sign language. Each little speed bump is really a learning opportunity in disguise!

recognizing baby's signs

There is one mistake I see parents and caregivers make over and over again, and I'm determined to make sure it doesn't happen to you. Here's what happens: You start signing with your baby and spend weeks (or months) diligently signing at every opportunity. Then, she starts signing back—and nobody notices!

How does this happen? It's actually easy to see where things might go wrong when you think about it. In the same way a baby's first word is typically a simplified version of a spoken word (like "muh muh" for *mommy*), a baby's first sign will likely be a close approximation of the sign, which can make it hard to know if it's a sign at all.

It's important to keep in mind that ASL signs are made up of three important components: handshape (the position of the hand), location (where on the body the sign is done), and movement (the motion of the sign). For example, for the sign for **MORE** (page 27), the handshape is fingers and thumbs touching for both hands (known as a "flat *O*" handshape), the location is in front of the body, and the movement is bringing the hands together two times. As adults, we can easily do all three of these things correctly and simultaneously. However, for a baby, getting all those pieces just right is tricky. Sometimes a baby will get the motion of a sign correct but not the location, or vice versa. Because babies are still developing their fine motor skills, handshape is generally limited to either an open hand or closed fist, or maybe just the pointer finger extended. Keep this in mind when watching for early signs.

I want to be sure you don't make this common mistake, so throughout this book, I've included tips to help you know what to look for. You'll find these tips alongside the instructions to most signs under the heading ◉ *What to look for*.

In addition, here are three clues that your baby is signing:

Clue #1 Purposeful and repetitive movement

If your baby starts moving his hands or arms in a repetitive way, there's a good chance he is signing. You might not know which sign he's doing, and that's okay. Just acknowledge the attempt so he knows you are paying attention. Encourage his attempt by commenting on his action and praising his effort. You can even try to guess the sign if you're not sure, based on the context and the signs you've been using regularly. "I see you moving your hands! Are you telling me something? What do you see? Do you see the **BALL** (page 33)?"

Clue #2 The direction of the baby's gaze

If your baby is gesturing with purpose and repetitively, follow her gaze to see what she might be looking at—this might lead you right to the answer. If her eyes seem fixed on something while she is making purposeful and repetitive movements, she is most likely signing!

Clue #3 Looking to you for a response

If you see your baby doing something repetitive with his hands or arms and he is looking at you expectantly, this is a strong indication that he's signing and waiting for you to respond. If you're not sure what sign it might be, again, make your best guess based on the context of the situation and movement of the sign.

So now you know what to look for. Be sure to acknowledge and encourage your baby's early signing attempts, even if you're not sure what sign it might be. Ignoring your little one might discourage her from trying, and we definitely don't want that!

top 5 useful signs

milk

Open and close your dominant hand (the hand you write with) a few times.

✳ Memory tip

It's as if you are milking a cow.

⏰ When to use the sign

If you think your baby is getting ready for a feeding, you can sign **MILK** and ask, "Do you want some **MILK**?" You can reinforce the sign further by signing and saying it while your baby is drinking milk, whether bottle- or breastfeeding.

👁 What to look for

Your baby's sign for **MILK** might look like she's waving to you. Or, if her hand is touching her body when she signs **MILK**, it might look like she's scratching an itch.

eat

Bring your fingers and thumb together and tap them to your lips a few times.

✳ Memory tip

It's like you're putting food into your mouth.

🕐 When to use the sign

EAT is a great sign to introduce when your baby starts eating solid food. Sign **EAT** when you suspect your baby is getting hungry and while he is eating. You can also sign **EAT** if he is watching you or a pet eating.

👁 What to look for

Your baby might sign this by sticking his finger (or even his whole hand) in his mouth. He might also pat his face or head.

🧩 Similar signs

The signs for **EAT** and **FOOD** are the same so you can use this sign interchangeably with both spoken words.

*My first daughter signed **EAT** by touching her open hand to her ear. I was new to signing and had no idea she was signing **EAT**. I thought she had an ear infection! One day she touched her ear immediately when I asked her if she wanted to **EAT** and it finally clicked that she was signing. Remember that babies will do their best to copy the signs you show them, but it's completely normal for their early attempts to be adorably imperfect.*

more

Bring your fingers and thumbs together on both hands and then tap the tips of your fingers together in front of your body.

✳ Memory tip

It's like you're adding things together each time your fingertips touch.

🕐 When to use the sign

MORE is often used when babies are eating: "Do you want **MORE**?" This causes some babies to think that **MORE** = **FOOD**, and they will start to sign **MORE** whenever they are hungry. To avoid this confusion, make sure to sign **MORE** when you are doing anything your baby enjoys, such as singing, bouncing, or even belly kisses! In time, your baby will start letting you know when she wants **MORE**, and not just when it comes to food.

👁 What to look for

Babies might sign **MORE** by clapping their hands or banging their fists together. Or they might touch their pointer finger to their opposite palm.

Parents often tell me that their babies use the sign for **MORE** *when they really want something, even after they start talking. As a young toddler, my own little one used to say and sign* **MORE** *for emphasis to let me know she was serious.*

all done

Start with your hands open and palms facing you, then twist your wrists so your palms are facing out. Repeat this motion a few times.

✳ Memory tip
It's like you're brushing something away from you.

🕐 **When to use the sign**
Use this sign whenever you wrap up an activity with your little one. You can ask, "Are you **ALL DONE**?" when you think he is done eating. Sign and say **ALL DONE** when you're about to take him out of the high chair, car seat, or bathtub. Before you know it, he will be letting you know when he's had enough by signing **ALL DONE** instead of fussing. You can also use this sign when you say "finished" or "the end."

👁 **What to look for**
Baby might sign this by waving or flapping one or both hands, or by sweeping his hands side to side.

bed

Tilt your head to the side and rest it on the palm of your open hand.

✳ **Memory tip**

It's like you're resting your head on a pillow.

🕐 **When to use the sign**

Say and sign **BED** whenever your baby is acting sleepy and every time you put her down for a nap and at bedtime. She will make the connection with the sign and start to let you know when she's feeling tired. You can also use this sign as an alternative to "sleep" or "sleepy."

❇ **Similar signs**

Sometimes you see this sign done with the head resting on both hands together (palms touching), which is another acceptable way to sign **BED**.

*My younger daughter would sign **BED** anytime she saw a baby sleeping and even when a character in a book had his or her eyes closed!*

top **5** playful signs

dog

Pat your thigh a few times.

✻ Memory tip

It's like you're calling a dog to come to you.

🕐 When to use the sign

Sign **DOG** when your pet is within sight. If you don't have a dog, sign **DOG** when you see one in the neighborhood or when visiting friends or family with one. You can also find lots of dogs in children's books!

DOG is a great sign to do on your baby's body at first. Just gently pat her thigh with her hand and say "dog" to help her get the idea.

❇ Similar signs

DOG can also be signed by snapping your fingers (like you are calling a dog to you) or by a combination of patting your thigh and snapping your fingers. Because patting the thigh is easiest for little ones, I recommend using that version. However, if you have a pet that has been trained to jump when you pat, feel free to make a snapping motion (with or without the sound) instead.

light

Touch all your fingers together and lift the back of your wrist up above your head. Open and close your fingers a few times.

✳ Memory tip

Opening your fingers is like light rays shining down on you.

⏰ When to use the sign

Introduce this sign by turning the light off and then on again, either with a lamp or light switch. Turn the lights on and say and sign **LIGHT**. Once your baby starts signing **LIGHT**, you'll realize that just about everything has a light!

👁 What to look for

Baby's version of **LIGHT** might look a lot like the sign for **MILK** (page 25), but most babies raise their arm when they sign **LIGHT**. If you're not sure which sign it is, pay attention to your baby's gaze and behavior. Is he looking at you, eager for a feeding? Or is he looking at something with a light on it?

🧩 Similar signs

This sign is the same as the second half of the sign for **SUN** (page 89).

LIGHT might not seem like an obvious first choice for baby signing, but it's hands down my favorite sign to start with. It was an early and favorite sign for both of my kids, and I've seen it help countless families get off to an early and strong start with signing. It goes back to what we discussed at the beginning of the chapter about working with your baby's interests. You'll be amazed at how quickly your little one picks up this sign. And once signing "clicks," you'll be able to introduce more practical signs with ease.

ball

Curve all the fingers of both hands and bring them toward each other a few times in front of your body.

✳ **Memory tip**

It's like showing the shape of an invisible ball.

🕐 **When to use the sign**

Balls are a fun and easy way to engage little ones in play. You can get a plush ball for a younger baby and a bouncy one for an older child. Pass the ball back and forth. Sign **BALL** while the baby is holding it. You can even do a modified version of the sign for **BALL** while holding the ball in one hand: Either do half of the sign with your free hand or bring your free hand onto the ball.

👁 **What to look for**

Babies might sign **BALL** by knocking their fists together or clapping. My younger daughter signed **BALL** by touching her closed fist to her opposite open hand.

*You might be surprised at the many ways your baby will use this sign. I have seen babies sign **BALL** to describe everything from ornaments on a Christmas tree to a picture of puffed cereal on a cereal box and even pumpkins in a pumpkin patch!*

book

Place your hands flat together and then open them outward.

✳ Memory tip

It's like you are opening a book.

⏰ When to use the sign

Let your baby hold a board book while you talk about it. Ask, "Are you reading the **BOOK**?" and "Do you want me to read the **BOOK** to you?" Sign **BOOK** whenever you are reading with your baby. Books are also a great resource for introducing new words and signs.

👁 What to look for

Your baby might sign **BOOK** by making one large clapping motion or by clasping her hands together. If you are using multiple signs that involve bringing the hands together, like **MORE** (page 27), **BALL** (page 33), and **SHOES** (page 63), you'll have to decide by the context which sign she is doing. Follow her gaze to see what she's looking at as a starting point.

car

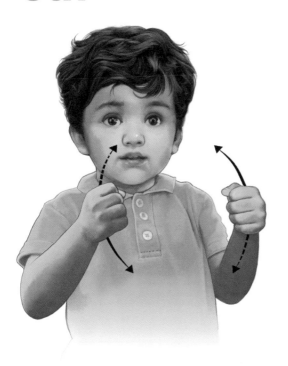

Place your fists in front of your body and move them up and down alternately in a circular motion.

✳ Memory tip

It's like you're turning the steering wheel of a car back and forth.

◷ When to use the sign

Sign **CAR** when you're getting in the car, when you're out for a walk and see cars zooming by, and when you see cars in a book.

Capture your baby's attention by making fun noises, like "beep beep" and "vroom vroom," when signing **CAR**.

👁 What to look for

Your baby might wave both hands up and down together (either open or closed in fists) instead of alternately.

🧩 Similar signs

The sign for **TRUCK** is very similar to **CAR**. Just hold your hands a little lower and spread them farther apart to show the bigger steering wheel of the truck.

SIGNING FUN

Here are some fun tools for practicing the first signs. Use songs, books, and activities as opportunities to sign with baby and make the learning process more enjoyable for you both.

Sign and Read:
Doggies by Sandra Boynton

I love using sign language during story time. It makes reading together more interactive and gives your baby an opportunity to participate. Incorporating signing into your story time takes a little bit of practice, but once you get the hang of it, you'll find it's a great opportunity to introduce new words and signs to your baby's growing vocabulary.

This simple board book by Sandra Boynton features a variety of dogs on every page, giving you lots of opportunities to practice signing **DOG** (page 31) over and over. It also has fun doggie sound effects! In addition to **DOG**, you can use this opportunity to practice signing **BOOK** (page 34) with your baby. Don't forget to sign **ALL DONE** (page 28) when you get to the last page!

Key Vocabulary

DOG, p. 31   **BOOK,** p. 34   **ALL DONE,** p. 28

Sign and Play:
Going for a Ride

When it's time to head out for a drive, tell your baby you're going for a ride in the **CAR** (page 35). Say and sign **CAR** again as you get her settled into her car seat. When you reach your destination, say and sign **ALL DONE** (page 28) as you take your baby out of the car. Simple but effective!

Key Vocabulary

CAR, p. 35   **ALL DONE,** p. 28

story time tips

Holding a board book and a squirmy baby is already a lot to handle—so how are you supposed to use your hands for signing, too? Don't worry, it's easier than you think! The following tips will help you get started:

- Pick sturdy books with bright photos and repetitive themes. You'll see my book suggestions in the Signing Fun section of each chapter, or you can skip ahead to Resources (page 143) for a complete list.

- Put the baby on your lap and hold the book with one hand or prop it up in front of you.

- As you read, sign key words in the space between the book and baby.

- You can also sign directly on the book. When the baby is looking at the page, sign right where she's looking. For instance, point to a dog and then sign **DOG** (page 31) so she makes the connection.

- You can also try signing on her body. Pat the baby's head when she notices some-one in the picture is wearing a hat, or gently rub her chest as you read about the bath.

- If your little one is too wriggly for these suggestions, try placing her in a high chair. Place the book on the chair's tray and sit face-to-face with the baby. This is particularly useful for great eye contact and incorporating facial expressions into your signing and storytelling.

Sign and Sing:
"The More We Get Together"

Signing and singing with your baby is a rewarding way to build signing into your daily routine and to expose him to both music and language. Little ones love music and learn from the rhythm and repetition of familiar tunes. You don't have to have a great singing voice to have a wonderful experience singing to your baby. Your voice is his favorite, so let go of any self-consciousness and sing your heart out!

This is a classic children's song that you might already know. If not, you can easily find a video on YouTube to learn the tune. When I sing this song with little ones, I use only three signs: **MORE** (page 27), **HAPPY** (page 132), and **FRIEND** (page 129). When you're just getting started, you can use just the sign for **MORE**, then add the other signs later.

The **MORE** we get together, together,

together,

The **MORE** we get together,

The **HAPPIER** we'll be,

'Cause my **FRIENDS** are your **FRIENDS,**

And your **FRIENDS** are my **FRIENDS.**

The **MORE** we get together,

The **HAPPIER** we'll be.

Key Vocabulary

MORE, p. 27   **HAPPY,** p. 132   **FRIEND,** p. 129

③

Mealtime and Manners

MEALTIME IS A GREAT TIME to practice signing. Once your baby has started solids and is trying new foods, you'll begin the process of discovering what your child likes—and doesn't. Your child is a captive audience at mealtime (literally, since he is strapped into a high chair), so you'll have both hands free to sign and can make good eye contact. Signing allows your baby to request his favorite foods and let you know when he's all done eating. It helps reduce the frustration that often accompanies this phase of infancy, and you'll likely end up with less food thrown on the floor as a result. Bonus!

In chapter 2, you learned some great mealtime signs to get started with, like **EAT** (page 26), **MORE** (page 27), **MILK** (page 25), and **ALL DONE** (page 28). In this chapter, you'll learn even more mealtime signs for the most common baby and toddler foods, like **APPLE** (page 42), **CHEESE** (page 45), and **CRACKER** (page 46). You might also find it helpful to use the sign for **HOT** (page 73) to let your baby know when food is too hot to eat.

In this chapter, you'll also learn how to sign **PLEASE** (page 50) and **THANK YOU** (page 51). While babies may not fully grasp the idea of manners, it's never too early to start practicing these important social skills.

banana

apple

Extend the pointer finger of your non-dominant hand. With your dominant hand, press your fingertips together and move them from the top to the bottom of your opposite pointer finger.

Close your hand (or make a fist) and lift your bent pointer finger so that it sticks out. Touch the knuckle of your pointer finger to your cheek, then twist it a few times.

✳ Memory tip

It's like you are peeling a banana.

✳ Memory tip

Your knuckle is touching the apple of your cheek.

◎ When to use the sign

Sign **BANANA** while your little monkey watches you cut or mash bananas, and sign it again while she is enjoying her banana.

◎ When to use the sign

Sign **APPLE** when your baby is eating an apple or applesauce, or when you see apples at the grocery store.

◉ What to look for

Baby might sign **BANANA** by brushing her pointer fingers or whole hands together.

◉ What to look for

The little one might tap his face with his finger or twist his pointer finger on his cheek.

pear

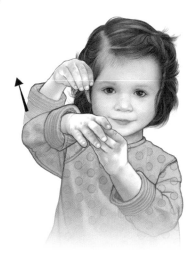

Start with your fingers and thumb of your nondominant hand touching. Cover those fingers with your dominant hand and then pull your dominant hand up and off your other hand.

✳ **Memory tip**
It's like you're hiding and revealing the shape of a pear.

🕐 **When to use the sign**
Sign **PEAR** when your little one is enjoying a sweet, juicy pear, whether puréed or cut up. If you have a whole pear handy, sign **PEAR** next to it to show her how the sign looks like the fruit. You can even modify the sign by signing with your dominant hand actually on the pear!

👁 **What to look for**
Baby might look like she is grabbing one hand with the other.

peach

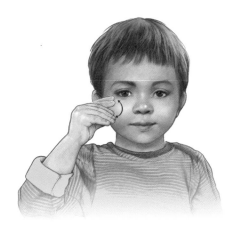

With one hand, gently touch your finger-tips to your cheek, bringing your fingers and thumb together as you stroke your cheek and move your hand away from your face.

✳ **Memory tip**
It's like you are feeling the peach fuzz on your face.

🕐 **When to use the sign**
Let your baby feel the fuzzy surface of the peach. Touch the peach yourself, then show your baby how to sign **PEACH**.

👁 **What to look for**
Baby might look like he is grabbing or brushing his face.

yogurt

Make a *Y* handshape (page 142) with your dominant hand and a *C* handshape (page 142) with your nondominant hand. Scoop the pinky finger of your *Y* hand into your *C* hand and bring your *Y* hand to your mouth.

✳ Memory tip

It's like your pinky finger is the spoon and your other hand is the container of yogurt. You are scooping the yogurt from the container into your mouth.

🕑 When to use the sign

Use this sign when your baby is eating yogurt from a spoon or from a squeezable pouch or tube.

👁 What to look for

Your baby might sign **YOGURT** by moving her pointer finger to her mouth.

cereal

Wiggle your pointer finger up and down as you move your finger across your chin.

✳ Memory tip

It's like you're wiping the milk that dribbled down your chin while eating cereal.

🕑 When to use the sign

You can use this sign when your baby is eating baby cereal, oatmeal, or dry cereal as finger food.

*By the time my babies were signing, they were mostly munching on dry cereal as a snack and not the "baby cereal" they ate as a first food. Because their favorite cereal to snack on was O shaped, we signed the letter O (page 142) instead of **CEREAL**, which worked well for our family. You might want to try it, too!*

egg

Start with both hands in a *U* handshape (page 142). With your dominant hand, knock the two fingers of your nondominant hand, and then move both hands down and apart.

✳ Memory tip

It's like you are cracking an egg, with your dominant hand "cracking" against your nondominant hand.

◷ When to use the sign

Sign **EGG** when your baby is eating eggs of any style: hardboiled, scrambled, you name it!

◉ What to look for

Your baby might tap two pointer fingers together or tap both hands together.

cheese

Place your palms together and twist them back and forth in opposite directions a few times.

✳ Memory tip

It's like you're squishing a flat slice of cheese.

◷ When to use the sign

If your baby loves cheese, this might become a favorite sign! Sign **CHEESE** whenever he is enjoying some.

◉ What to look for

It might look like your baby is clapping or pretending to wash his hands.

*This is a popular sign for many babies! So many of my students have shared pictures and funny stories about their little one signing **CHEESE** in family photos. Say **CHEESE**!*

bread

Start with your nondominant hand in front of you, palm facing you. Then move the fingertips of your dominant hand in downward "slices" from top to bottom along the back of your non-dominant hand.

✱ Memory tip
It's like you're slicing a loaf of bread.

🕐 When to use the sign
Use the sign for **BREAD** when making toast, eating bread, or making a sandwich.

👁 What to look for
Your baby might brush her hands together or drag only her pointer finger across either side of the opposite hand.

cracker

Make fists with both hands and knock the fist of your dominant hand twice on the elbow of your nondominant arm.

✱ Memory tip
It's like you are "cracking" wheat to make crackers.

🕐 When to use the sign
You can use the sign **CRACKER** for any salty or crunchy snack food. If your little one is like most babies, this will quickly become a favorite sign.

👁 What to look for
Many babies sign **CRACKER** by knocking their fist on their opposite hand or wrist.

One day my daughter made a loud noise while I was out with her in the stroller. I looked around to see what was wrong only to find her enthusiastically signing **CRACKER**. *She had "shouted" just loud enough to get my attention. I was so glad she did that and then had the tools to let me know what she wanted, instead of fussing and crying.*

pasta

Start with your pinky fingers touching, then move them away from each other in a spiral motion.

✳ **Memory tip**

It's like you are drawing swirly spaghetti with your fingers.

🕐 **When to use the sign**

While this sign looks like spaghetti, you can use it for any form of pasta or noodles.

👁 **What to look for**

If very young, your baby might start this sign with his pointers touching, rather than pinkies.

meat

With your dominant hand, pinch the flesh between the thumb and pointer finger of your opposite hand.

✳ **Memory tip**

It's like you're pinching the "meaty" part of your hand.

🕐 **When to use the sign**

You can use the sign **MEAT** when your baby is eating chicken, pork, beef, or any kind of animal protein.

👁 **What to look for**

It might look like your baby is grabbing at her hand or arm.

potato

Make a bent *V* handshape (page 142) with your dominant hand and a fist with your opposite hand. Tap the fingertips of the bent *V* on the back of your opposite fist.

✳ Memory tip

It's like poking a potato with a fork to check if it's done.

◷ When to use the sign

Use the sign for **POTATO** when your baby eats potatoes cooked in any way: mashed, baked, or fried!

◉ What to look for

Baby might tap his fingertips on his opposite open hand or fist.

carrot

Start with your closed fist next to your mouth and move it downward.

✳ Memory tip

It's like you bit a piece off the carrot and are still holding the rest of it.

◷ When to use the sign

This is a fun sign to exaggerate with a big biting motion and crunching noise. Baby will have fun mimicking your silly version of the sign.

◉ What to look for

If you play up this sign with a dramatic crunch, you'll be in for a treat when your baby starts mimicking you with her own adorable version of **CARROT**.

cookie

Bend all the fingers of your dominant hand (this is called a "claw" handshape in ASL). Tap and twist the fingertips of your "claw" hand on the open palm of your opposite hand.

✳ **Memory tip**

It's like your "claw" hand is a cookie cutter and you are cutting dough on a cookie sheet.

🕐 **When to use the sign**

You might be worried about teaching this one, but don't be! Baby will likely pick it up quickly, and use it often, but that's actually a good thing. A request for a **COOKIE** can let you know your baby is hungry, and then you can offer other options. You can say, "I know you want a **COOKIE**. Let's **EAT** (page 26) some lunch and maybe we can have a **COOKIE** later."

👁 **What to look for**

At first, it might look like your baby is clapping or tapping his fingertips to the opposite hand or arm.

water

Make a *W* handshape (page 142) and tap it on your chin a few times.

✳ **Memory tip**

Water starts with *W*.

🕐 **When to use the sign**

Sign **WATER** when your baby starts drinking water from a sippy cup. You can also sign **WATER** when giving your baby a bath or if you see any body of water—from a small puddle to a large lake. **WATER** is also a good sign to add to **DRINK** (page 50).

👁 **What to look for**

Most babies and toddlers don't yet have the fine motor control to form the *W* handshape for this sign so will likely sign this with all fingers or just a pointer finger.

drink

Make a C handshape (page 142) and tip it at your lips.

✳ Memory tip

It's like you're taking a sip from an invisible glass.

🕐 When to use the sign

DRINK is a great sign to introduce when your baby starts drinking from a sippy cup. When she signs **DRINK**, you'll know she's thirsty.

👁 What to look for

Baby might touch her mouth or wave her hand away from her mouth.

please

Rub your flat hand in a circular motion on your chest.

✳ Memory tip

It's like you are rubbing your heart because you want something so much.

🕐 When to use the sign

Teach your baby the sign for **PLEASE** by modeling it yourself when you want him to give you something. Or, if he wants something, you can ask him to "say **PLEASE**" and pause a moment before giving the desired object. Don't withhold things for long, though—you don't want to frustrate your baby.

👁 What to look for

Babies often look like they are wiping or rubbing their chest when they sign **PLEASE**.

✿ Similar signs

SORRY (page 135) is very similar to **PLEASE** but is done with a closed fist. When you sign **SORRY**, your facial expression should indicate *sorry*, too.

thank you

Place the fingers of your flat hand on your chin, then move your hand away.

✳ **Memory tip**

It's like returning the favor when someone gives you something.

🕐 **When to use the sign**

Sign **THANK YOU** to your baby whenever she hands you something or does something you request (like sit down). With time, she will get the idea and sign **THANK YOU** when you give her something!

👁 **What to look for**

Your baby might touch or tap her mouth, which could look like she's signing **EAT** (page 26).

🧩 **Similar signs**

The sign for **GOOD** is similar to **THANK YOU**. However, when signing **GOOD**, the hand moving away from your chin lands on your opposite open palm.

I remember grocery shopping with my first baby—I would give her cereal to keep her happy in the shopping cart. She would often sign **THANK YOU** *after I gave her a snack. Passersby would think she was blowing kisses and would wave or blow kisses back. I never corrected them—they probably wouldn't have believed me anyway!*

SIGNING FUN

Sign and Sing:
"Apples and Bananas"

Now that you've learned mealtime signs, practice them with a riff on the traditional children's song "Apples and Bananas." This song normally teaches vowel sounds, but you'll be teaching food signs. Have fun and substitute your child's favorite foods.

Key Vocabulary

EAT, p. 26   **APPLE,** p. 42   **BANANA,** p. 42

CHEESE, p. 45   **CRACKER,** p. 46   **CEREAL,** p. 44

YOGURT, p. 44

I like to **EAT**, **EAT**, **EAT APPLES** and

BANANAS.

(repeat two times)

I like to **EAT**, **EAT**, **EAT CHEESE** and

CRACKERS.

(repeat two times)

I like to **EAT**, **EAT**, **EAT** Cheerios (sign

CEREAL) and **YOGURT.**

(repeat two times)

Sign and Read:
The Very Hungry Caterpillar by Eric Carle

This classic book is perfect for practicing the sign for **EAT** (page 26). That little caterpillar just eats everything! You can use just the sign for **EAT**, or you can practice the signs for **APPLE** (page 42), **PEAR** (page 43), and **CHEESE** (page 45). As your baby's signing vocabulary grows, you can also sign **EGG** (page 45), **MOON** (page 76), **SUN** (page 89), **BUG** (for "caterpillar"; page 91), and **BUTTERFLY** (page 92). Remember, the signs for **EAT** and **FOOD** are the same, so you use that sign for both words.

Key Vocabulary

BUG, p. 91   **MOON,** p. 76   **EGG,** p. 44

SUN, p. 89   **EAT,** p. 28   **APPLE,** p. 42

PEAR, p. 43   **CHEESE,** p. 45   **BUTTERFLY,** p. 92

Sign and Play:
This or That?

One of the best things about teaching your baby signs for foods is that it allows him to actually ask for specific foods.

To help build your baby's signing vocabulary for foods, I recommend a game called "This or That?" The idea is simple: Give baby the option between two foods you would like him to learn the signs for. Overemphasize the spoken word and signs to give him ample time to hear and see the options. For example, ask your baby, "Do you want **CHEESE** (page 45)? Or do you want **APPLES** (page 42)?"

Give baby a chance to respond, but don't frustrate him. If he grabs for the preferred food, reinforce the sign for that word. Say, "Oh, you really want the **CHEESE**! You took the **CHEESE** right out of my hand. You love **CHEESE**, don't you?"

Play this game regularly to introduce new signs and practice ones you already know.

Key Vocabulary

CHEESE, p. 45   **APPLE,** p. 42

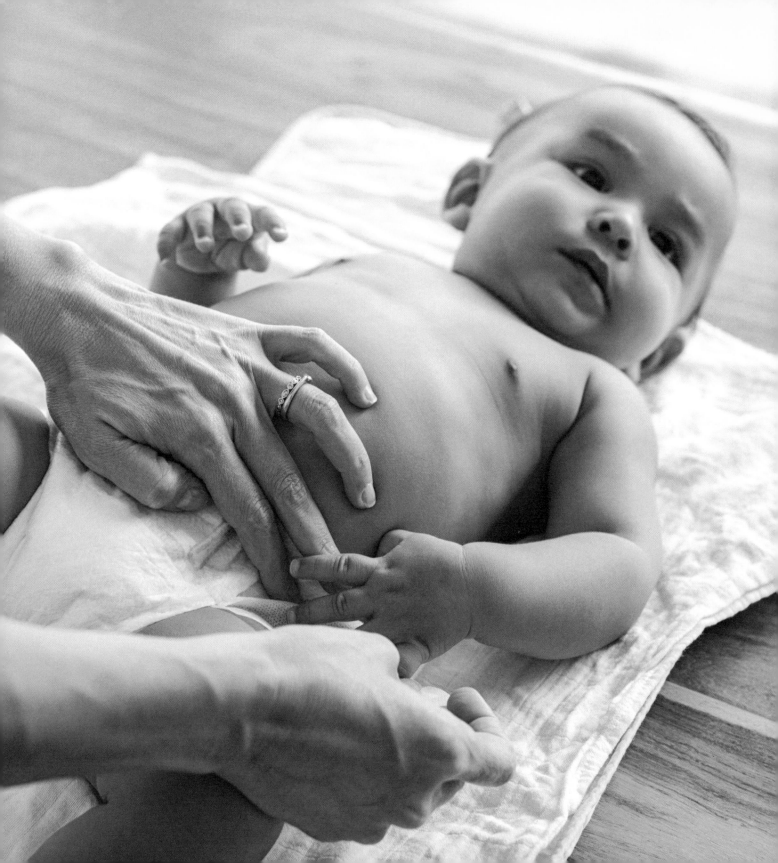

4

Change Me and Getting Dressed

F ALL THE THINGS you do with your baby each day, changing diapers is one thing you can count on doing over and over (and over). It's a great opportunity to incorporate a few chosen signs and make them part of your routine.

Some babies loathe diaper changes. If this sounds like your little one, learning diaper-related signs probably won't be high on her priority list. Instead, you can use this part of the day to practice other signs. For example, tape some photos of **GRANDMA** (page 127) and **GRANDPA** (page 127) near the changing table, and practice those signs while you're changing baby. Or keep a little **BALL** (page 33) or toy **CAR** (page 35) handy for your baby to hold while you're changing her, and practice those signs instead. You might also want to teach your baby signs for clothes. You may find that baby is most interested in the things she can pull off herself, like **HATS** (page 61), **SOCKS** (page 62), and **SHOES** (page 63). Choose the signs you think will be the most useful to you or that you and your baby will have the most fun with.

diaper

With both hands at your hips, and first two fingers together, open and close your first two fingers and your thumb.

✳ Memory tip

It's like you're showing where a diaper fastens.

◎ When to use the sign

If you want to teach your baby the sign for **DIAPER**, make sure he can see it. You might try signing **DIAPER** on a stuffed animal or doll that is wearing a diaper instead of on yourself. In order to help your baby see the sign for **DIAPER**, you can modify the sign by moving your hands up closer to your face to make it more visible.

✿ Similar signs

The sign for **CHANGE** also works great as an alternative to **DIAPER**, as it is easier to sign in your baby's line of sight.

👁 What to look for

It might look like your baby is waving with both hands or patting himself on the belly or hips.

change

Stack your closed fists on top of each other with your fingers touching. Flip your hands so the one that was on the bottom is now on top.

✳ Memory tip

Your hands "change" position with each other.

◎ When to use the sign

This is a great sign to use when changing your baby's diaper. The sign for **DIAPER** is signed at the hips, which may be difficult for her to see. **CHANGE** is a great alternative as you can sign it right in your baby's line of sight as you prepare to change her diaper.

potty

Make a *T* handshape (page 142) with your dominant hand and shake it slightly from side to side.

✻ Memory tip

T stands for *toilet*. However, with babies and toddlers, this sign is often paired with the word *potty*. It's up to you which spoken word you use with this sign.

🕐 When to use the sign

POTTY is a great sign to introduce when little ones begin to learn to use the potty. It is also useful if you are practicing "elimination communication," which is when caregivers try to recognize and respond to babies' cues in order to enable them to pee or poop in a toilet or other receptacle.

👁 What to look for

At first, this sign might look like a little wave of the fist.

My girls are both school-age now, but their school uses this sign in the classroom for students to discreetly request to be excused. It's a useful sign for all ages to be able to communicate privately about needing to use the bathroom, or from a distance if you're at the playground or in a noisy environment.

poop

Make a thumbs-up sign with your dominant hand and wrap your nondominant fist around the thumb. Then pull your thumb downward out of the fist.

✳ **Memory tip**
This one really needs no explanation.

◎ **When to use the sign**
You can sign **POOP** when you suspect that's what your baby's up to. You can also use this sign when he starts pooping on the potty.

◉ **What to look for**
It might look like clasping hands together and then pulling them apart.

clean

Put your nondominant hand flat out in front of you, palm facing up. Swipe your dominant hand across your bottom hand with palms touching, moving from wrist to fingertips.

✳ **Memory tip**
It's like you're wiping crumbs off a table.

◎ **When to use the sign**
Sign **CLEAN** once your baby is clean and dry.

◉ **What to look for**
Your baby might wipe her hands together in an exaggerated way.

✿ **Similar signs**
The sign for **CLEAN** is the same as **NICE**, so you can use this sign with both spoken words interchangeably.

dirty

Place the back of your dominant hand under your chin and wiggle all of your fingers.

✳ **Memory tip**

It's like dirt and food dripping from your chin.

🕐 **When to use the sign**

Sign **DIRTY** when your baby needs a diaper change or when his face or hands are dirty. You can also sign **DIRTY** when his clothes are wet or dirty.

👁 **What to look for**

It might look like your baby is grabbing at or gently scratching his face.

✹ **Similar signs**

The sign for **PIG** (page 113) is quite similar, except when signing **PIG**, the whole hand bends and the fingers move downward together.

wash hands

Rub your hands together.

✳ **Memory tip**

It's like you're washing your hands.

🕐 **When to use the sign**

You can sign **WASH HANDS** when you wash your baby's hands or clean them with a wipe. You can also do this sign when she is watching you wash your hands.

*When my second daughter was about 18 months old, we decided to bring her big sister's play kitchen down from the attic. She was so excited! The first thing she did was toddle over to it, point to the little sink, and sign **WASH HANDS**.*

clothes

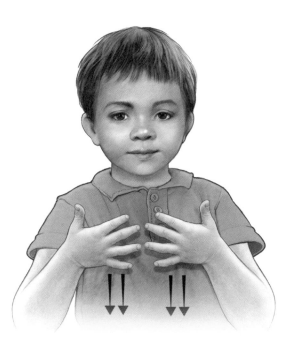

With both hands open and palms facing you, brush your upper chest in a downward motion.

✳ **Memory tip**

It's like you're smoothing out the clothes you just put on.

🕐 **When to use the sign**

Sign **CLOTHES** when you are getting your baby dressed for the day. You can say, "Are you ready to get dressed? Let's put on your **CLOTHES** now."

👁 **What to look for**

It might look like your baby is wiping or rubbing her body.

🧩 **Similar signs**

The sign for **CLOTHES** is the same as **GET DRESSED**, so you can sign **CLOTHES** when talking about getting dressed or putting on your clothes.

hat

Pat the top of your head with your flat hand.

* **Memory tip**

It's like you're showing exactly where a hat goes.

🕐 **When to use the sign**

This is such a fun and easy sign to teach your baby. I highly recommend introducing it early on. You can sign **HAT** on your own head or right on your baby's head. You can also sign **HAT** when either one of you puts on your own hat.

👁 **What to look for**

Babies usually pick this one up quickly. It's so easy, it will probably look like your version right away.

🧩 **Similar signs**

There are variations for different types of hats, such as baseball caps, party hats, and winter knit caps. I recommend just sticking with this general sign for **HAT**.

*My first daughter would sign **HAT** whenever she saw something that she thought was interesting on someone's head. If someone had a large hair bow, a hoodie, or one time even a big Mohawk, she would sign **HAT** to let me know what she was observing.*

socks

Point your index fingers at the floor and brush them against each other as you move them up and down alternately.

✻ Memory tip

It's like knitting needles knitting warm, woolly socks.

When to use the sign

Sign **SOCKS** when putting on your baby's socks or when you see him playing with his socks. You can also introduce this sign when playing Dress Up Bear (page 67) at the end of this chapter.

What to look for

Most babies develop the ability to point around their first birthday. Even so, your little one might not get the hang of making this pointing hand-shape while signing for some time. Therefore, early versions of this sign might be made with open hands brushing together.

Both my babies loved to pull their socks off, especially when riding in the car. If you're not in a rush, take the opportunity to sign ***SOCKS*** *as you put your baby's socks back on. If he really doesn't want his socks on, he might just sign back* ***ALL DONE*** *(page 28) to let you know how he feels about it.*

shoes

Make fists with both hands with your palms facing the floor. Gently knock your fists together a few times.

✳ Memory tip

It's like you're banging your shoes together to knock off the dirt.

🕐 When to use the sign

Sign **SHOES** when putting on your baby's shoes. If your little one likes to pull her shoes off, you can say, "**WHERE** (page 86) is your **SHOE**?"

👁 What to look for

Your little one's version of **SHOES** might look a lot like **MORE** (page 27) if you teach her both of these signs. They both involve bringing the hands together in front of the body. You will be able to sort out which sign she is doing by the context, so don't worry about using these similar signs as they are both fun and useful.

My first daughter loved to walk around in my shoes or slippers as a young toddler and would sign SHOES to let me know how excited she was!

coat

Start with your fists at your shoulders and then slide them down your chest.

✳ **Memory tip**

It looks like you're pulling on your coat.

🕐 **When to use the sign**

Sign **COAT** as you're putting on your baby's coat to head outside. You can also use this sign for other outerwear, like bunting or snowsuits.

👁 **What to look for**

It might look like your baby is signing **BATH** (page 71), as both signs involve moving closed fists on the upper chest. Pay attention to the context and you'll quickly figure out what he means.

pants

Start with your hands flat against either side of the top of one leg, then move them down your thigh. Repeat this motion on your other leg.

✷ Memory tip

It's like you're showing the legs of your pants.

◉ What to look for

It might look like your baby is brushing or wiping his leg.

✸ Similar signs

Another way to sign **PANTS** is to start with both fists at your thighs and pull them up together to your waist, like you are pulling up your pants.

shirt

Pinch the fabric of your shirt in front of your shoulder.

✷ Memory tip

It's like you're showing exactly what your shirt is.

◕ When to use the sign

Sign **SHIRT** when putting on your baby's shirt. You can sign **SHIRT** on yourself just before you pull it over your baby's head, then sign **SHIRT** on her shirt once it's on. "Now you've got a shirt on, too!"

◉ What to look for

It might look like your baby is grabbing or pulling at her clothing.

SIGNING FUN

Sign and Sing:
"Change Your Diaper"

(Sung to the tune of "Oh My Darling, Clementine")

I love this classic tune because you can put just about any words to it that you want. This is an example of how to use it during a diaper change, but you could just as easily use it at mealtime to sign "**EAT** (page 26) your **CARROTS** (page 48), **EAT** your **CARROTS** . . ." The options are endless!

Key Vocabulary

CHANGE, p. 56   **DIAPER,** p. 56   **CLEAN,** p. 58

CHANGE your **DIAPER**, **CHANGE**

your **DIAPER**,

CHANGE your **DIAPER** 'cause it's wet.

I am gonna **CHANGE** your **DIAPER**

So you will be nice and **CLEAN**.

Sign and Read:
Blue Hat, Green Hat by Sandra Boynton

This book is perfect for teaching babies the signs for clothes! It features colorful illustrations, rhythmic text, and just enough silliness to make it fun. You'll have opportunities to sign **HAT** (page 61), **SOCKS** (page 62), **SHOES** (page 63), and more as animals show off their outfits. Plus you'll get a kick out of the silly turkey who just can't seem to get anything on the right way.

Key Vocabulary

HAT, p. 61   **SHIRT,** p. 65   **PANTS,** p. 65

COAT, p. 64   **SOCKS,** p. 62   **SHOES,** p. 63

Sign and Play:
Dress Up Bear

A great way to teach baby signs for clothing is to play "dress up" with a stuffed animal or baby doll. Take a favorite teddy **BEAR** (page 115) or doll and put your baby's socks and shoes on it. Talk about the **SOCKS** (page 62) and **SHOES** (page 63) as she touches and pulls on them. Take a hat and place it on the teddy bear and sign **HAT** (page 61) right on the bear. Then take the hat and put it on your own head. Your baby will be interested to see the hat on your head! Say and sign **HAT** with the hat on your head. You can also pat your baby's head and sign and say **HAT** to help her know where the sign goes on her own body. Have fun playing with clothing items and building up your little one's vocabulary.

Key Vocabulary

BEAR, p. 115   **SOCKS,** p. 62   **SHOES,** p. 63

HAT, p. 61

5

Bath Time and Bedtime

BATH TIME AND BEDTIME are filled with rituals that offer comforting predictability and quality up-close time.

You'll learn some great bath time signs in this chapter, like **BATH** (page 71), **BUBBLES** (page 72), **HOT** (page 73), and **COLD** (page 73). If you have a rubber **DUCK** (page 111) or other bath toys, you can look for the signs for them in chapters 6 and 7. You'll probably want to practice these signs *before* your baby is in the tub since you'll have your hands full. If you need one of your hands to support your baby in the tub, you can always modify signs as needed to sign with one hand.

Bedtime and naptime are things babies experience every day, multiple times a day, so why not add some signs into these regular activities? You've already learned some excellent signs for bedtime, like **BED** (page 29), **LIGHT** (page 32), and **BOOK** (page 34) in chapter 2. In this chapter, you'll learn how to sign **BRUSH TEETH** (page 75), **BLANKET** (page 75), **MOON** (page 76), and **STAR** (page 77), as well as two fun end-of-day activities for your bedtime routine.

bath time signs

bath

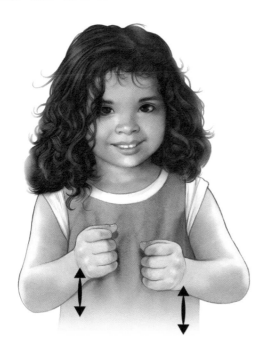

Make fists with both hands and gently rub your chest.

✳ **Memory tip**

It's like you're washing your body in the bath.

🕐 **When to use the sign**

Sign **BATH** when you start running the water for a bath. During bath time, when you may be using one hand to support your baby, you can modify the sign by doing it with your other hand on either yourself or the baby. When it's time to get out and dry off, don't forget to sign **ALL DONE** (page 28)!

👁 **What to look for**

It might look like your baby is wiping his body with open hands.

When my first baby was about 16 months old, we bought a small water table for her to play with out on the deck in the summer. When my husband first took it out of the box and popped it together, before we even added water, my daughter climbed in it, sat down, and signed **BATH**. *It was hilarious!*

bubbles

With both hands, make the O handshape (page 142), then open them as you alternate raising each hand.

✳ **Memory tip**

It's like bubbles floating up into the air and popping.

⏰ **When to use the sign**

Babies love bubbles, so this is a really fun and motivating sign to teach. Most babies will naturally reach up to try and touch the "bubbles," which is a great opportunity to cheer them on even though they may not be making the sign. As they reach for the bubbles, you can say, "That's right! **BUBBLES**! Good job signing. Catch the **BUBBLES** with your hands. Pop!"

👁 **What to look for**

It might look like your baby is waving or signing **MILK** (page 25) or **LIGHT** (page 32) with both hands.

In my classes, I blow bubbles at the end of each class. I always know the biggest bubbles fans because they start signing **BUBBLES** *as soon as they see me!*

hot

Place your dominant hand in front of your mouth with all your fingers curved in toward your mouth, then very quickly twist your hand around away from your mouth.

✳ **Memory tip**

It's like you're quickly taking something too hot out of your mouth and throwing it away.

◎ **When to use the sign**

Sign **HOT** if the water is too hot to get in the tub. You can also sign **HOT** when food is too warm to eat or as a warning not to touch the stove. You can introduce this sign safely by letting your baby touch something warm (like the outside of a bowl with warm food) and sign **HOT** so she understands the sensation. Of course, be very careful about this, and use common sense!

cold

Hold your arms close to your body with closed fists and shake them quickly.

✳ **Memory tip**

It's like you're shivering from the cold.

◎ **When to use the sign**

Sign **COLD** if your baby is shivering or when you're drying him off after the bath. Like introducing the sign for **HOT**, you can let your baby quickly touch something cold (like a bag of frozen peas or a chilled teether) and sign **COLD** so he understands the sensation.

◉ **What to look for**

Babies tend to nail this one! It's such a natural reaction to feeling cold that they often pick up this sign pretty easily.

There's nothing cuter than a freshly bathed baby doing the sign for **COLD***!*

bedtime signs

brush teeth

Place your pointer finger in front of your teeth and move it up and down.

* Memory tip

It's like your finger is your toothbrush.

When to use the sign

Let your baby hold his toothbrush while you demonstrate the sign for **BRUSH TEETH**. Have fun and make silly faces as you thoroughly **BRUSH TEETH** with your finger!

What to look for

Baby will likely poke his finger in his mouth.

blanket

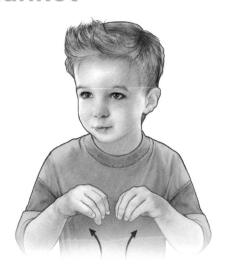

Start with your fingers pointing down in front of your body. Bring your fingers and your thumbs together and pull your hands up toward your chest.

* Memory tip

It's like you're pulling up a blanket.

When to use the sign

BLANKET is a helpful sign if your baby has a "lovey." If you think she wants her lovey, say, "Do you want your **BLANKET**?"

What to look for

It might look like your baby is rubbing her chest with both hands or tucking a fist under her chin.

moon

Make a modified C handshape
(page 142) with just your pointer
and thumb and touch it to your
cheek, then move it up and
away from your face.

✳ Memory tip

It's like you're placing the crescent moon up in
the sky.

🕐 When to use the sign

The sign for **MOON** can be used when reading
bedtime stories, like *Goodnight Moon*, *Kitten's
First Full Moon*, and *Papa, Please Get the Moon
for Me*. Of course, you can also sign **MOON** if you
see the real thing in the night sky!

👁 What to look for

It might look like your baby is pointing at the sky.

star

Lift both hands above your head with the pointer fingers extended. Brush your pointer fingers against each other as you alternately raise your hands up toward the sky.

✳ **Memory tip**

It's like you're pointing at all the stars in the sky.

🕐 **When to use the sign**

Sign **STAR** whenever you see a star shape. You might see stars in books about bedtime or nighttime, but you'll also find star shapes in lots of different places.

👁 **What to look for**

It might look like your baby is rubbing his hands together or pointing at the sky.

*My first daughter combined the sign for **STAR** with the sign for **FAN** (page 85) to describe the mobile hanging over her crib. It kind of blew my mind!*

SIGNING FUN

Sign and Sing:
"Twinkle, Twinkle, Little Star"

Babies love this song and its familiar tune (which happens to be the same melody as "Baa, Baa, Black Sheep" and the "ABC Song"). When I sign and sing this song, I sign **STAR** (page 77) over and over for the whole first line. To add the sign for UP, simply point your pointer finger up at the sky. Easy.

Key Vocabulary

STAR, p. 77   **WHAT,** p. 86

Twinkle, twinkle, little **STAR,**

How I wonder **WHAT** you are!

Up above the world so high,

Like a diamond in the sky.

Twinkle, twinkle, little **STAR,**

How I wonder **WHAT** you are!

Sign and Read:
The Going to Bed Book
by Sandra Boynton

There's no shortage of great bedtime stories for babies, but this one is my absolute favorite. The text has a wonderful rhythm to it, making it fun to read, and it's full of classic Boynton silliness. But what I especially love about this book is the way it goes through the process of winding down and getting ready for bed. It also has opportunities to practice many of the bath and bedtime signs you've learned in the chapter. The last page will leave both you and your baby ready to drift off as you rock him to sleep.

Key Vocabulary

BED, p. 29   **SUN,** p. 89   **BATH,** p. 71

BRUSH TEETH, p. 75   **MOON,** p. 76   **LIGHT,** p. 32

Sign and Play:
More Bubbles!

Take bath time up a notch: Keep some bubbles handy near the tub and blow them to entertain your baby. Sign **BUBBLES** (page 72) as you watch them float around. After all the bubbles have popped, ask, "Do you want **MORE** (page 27) **BUBBLES**?"

Your little one might reach up to try and touch the bubbles. Use this to your advantage, as reaching up and grabbing at the bubbles looks a lot like the actual sign for **BUBBLES**. As she reaches up to touch the bubbles, sign **BUBBLES** and say, "Good job! That's right— **BUBBLES**! We can say **BUBBLES** with our hands!" This will encourage her to sign by pointing out that her hand movements have meaning.

When it's time to put the bubbles away, let her know by signing **ALL DONE** (page 28) to the bubbles.

Key Vocabulary

MORE, p. 27   **BUBBLES,** p. 72   **ALL DONE,** p. 28

Sign and Play:
Goodnight, House

As mentioned in chapter 2, **LIGHT** (page 32) is an amazingly effective sign to get your baby interested in signing. For a fun way to teach your baby this sign, simply say and sign **LIGHT** as you turn the light on and off in each room at bedtime. You can do the same thing with the sign for **FAN** (page 85) if your house has ceiling fans or table fans. Say and sign **ALL DONE** (page 28) when you've finished saying goodnight to your house.

Key Vocabulary

LIGHT, p. 32   **FAN,** p. 85   **ALL DONE,** p. 28

6

Playtime and Out and About

THERE'S NO BETTER TIME to engage a baby in signing than during playtime! Playtime might just be a few short minutes, but those minutes can be powerful.

You've already learned some great playful signs in chapter 2, including **BALL** (page 33), **BOOK** (page 34) , and **CAR** (page 35). In this chapter, you'll learn more playtime signs, like **PLAY** (page 83) and **MUSIC** (page 84). You'll also learn how to sign **WHAT** (page 86) and **WHERE** (page 86), which you'll find useful in all sorts of games and activities (you'll find some suggestions for these at the end of this chapter).

As your little one grows and becomes more interested in the world around her, you'll want to introduce signs for the fascinating things you find when you go for a walk. In previous chapters, you've learned the nature signs **MOON** (page 76) and **STAR** (page 77). Now, in this chapter, you'll learn how to sign **TREE** (page 90), **BUG** (page 91), **SWING** (page 94), **BUS** (page 96), **AIRPLANE** (page 96), and more!

playtime signs

play

Make a *Y* handshape (page 142) with both hands and twist them away from each other.

✳ Memory tip

Think of your pinky and thumbs as little kids running all over the place and having a great time.

⏰ When to use the sign

PLAY is a great sign to use when your baby is in a good mood and you are having fun together. Use this sign when he has a toy or you are playing with him. You can say something like, "You are having so much fun **PLAYING** with that shape sorter! This toy is fun to **PLAY** with!"

👁 What to look for

The *Y* handshape is tricky, so your baby might just twist or shake his fists or pointer fingers excitedly.

🧩 Similar signs

If you make the same handshapes, but twist them side to side together in the same direction (instead of away from each other), that is the sign for **PARTY**.

music

Swing your dominant hand back and forth over the forearm of your nondominant hand.

✱ **Memory tip**

It's like you're conducting an orchestra.

🕐 **When to use the sign**

You can sign **MUSIC** when you're listening to music, while singing to your baby, or even if the ringtone on your phone plays a tune. You can also sign **MUSIC** each night when you sing a lullaby.

👁 **What to look for**

Baby will likely wave or swing one or both arms back and forth. It might look similar to her sign for **ALL DONE** (page 28), so pay attention to context to determine which sign it is.

🧩 **Similar signs**

The sign for **MUSIC** is the same as the sign for **SING**, so you can use this sign with both spoken words.

*When my second daughter was 16 months old, I was singing to her as I was putting on her pajamas after a bath. She signed **ALL DONE-MUSIC** to me . . . basically telling me, "Thanks but no thanks." I couldn't help but laugh!*

fan

Draw a circle in the air with your pointer finger.

✳ Memory tip

You're showing the ceiling fan spinning around and around.

🕐 When to use the sign

If you have a ceiling fan, turn it on, point at it, and sign **FAN**. You can also use this sign with a table-top or floor fan by pointing at the fan. This sign is directional, so with a fan that's facing you, you want to point your finger toward the fan, not the ceiling.

👁 What to look for

Baby will likely be looking at the fan and waving or pointing while moving his hand in a twist-ing motion.

We don't have ceiling fans at home, but a lot of big stores do. My daughters had fun looking up from the shopping carts for ceiling fans at stores like Costco. IKEA has huge ceiling fans!

what

Shrug your shoulders and, with both palms facing up, move your hands from side to side.

✱ **Memory tip**
This is a common gesture for asking someone the question, "What?"

◎ **When to use the sign**
This is a great sign to use if you don't know the sign for something but you want to use one. If your baby shows you something and you don't know the sign for it, you can say, "**WHAT** is it? **WHAT** do you have? Do you have a block?"

👁 **What to look for**
This one usually looks just like you would expect. And it's so cute when babies sign **WHAT**—they look so expressive!

where

Move your pointer finger from side to side.

✱ **Memory tip**
It's like you're asking, "Is it here or there?"

◎ **When to use the sign**
WHERE is a fun sign to use when playing hide-and-seek. Let your baby watch you hide a toy under a burp cloth or blanket, then ask her, "**WHERE** is it?" Pull the cloth off and say, "There it is!"

👁 **What to look for**
It might look like your baby is shaking her finger or hand.

nature signs

outside

Start with your hand loosely open at your shoulder, then close all your fingers as you move your hand away from your body two times.

🕐 **When to use the sign**

Sign **OUTSIDE** as you're getting ready to go play outside or go for a walk. Ask your baby, "Do you want to go **OUTSIDE**? Let's go **OUTSIDE**!"

👁 **What to look for**

It might look like your baby is moving his hand toward the door or grabbing at his shoulder.

rain

Start with your hands above your shoulders, palms facing forward and fingers spread open and relaxed. Then bend both your wrists downward as your arms move downward and repeat a few times.

✳ **Memory tip**

It's like you're showing sheets of rain falling down.

🕐 **When to use the sign**

Sign **RAIN** if you're out in the rain or reading a book that shows rain. It's fun to sign **RAIN** when singing "The Itsy Bitsy Spider," (page 97) too! You'll find this song at the end of this chapter.

👁 **What to look for**

It might look like your baby is waving both hands up and down.

sun

With your pointer finger,
draw a circle in the air and
then open all your fingers
toward your face.

✳ **Memory tip**

It's like you're drawing a picture of the sun in
the sky, with the rays of sunshine beaming
down on you.

🕐 **When to use the sign**

There are lots of bright yellow suns to be found in
board books and children's art, so take a moment
to point them out and sign **SUN**. I used this sign
often with my daughters because my favorite
song to sing to them was "You Are My Sunshine."

👁 **What to look for**

If your baby is already signing **LIGHT** (page 32),
her sign for **SUN** might look very similar.

🧩 **Similar signs**

The second half of this sign is the same as the sign
for **LIGHT** (page 32).

tree

Place your nondominant hand parallel to the floor, palm facing down. Then place the elbow of your dominant hand on your opposite hand, palm facing forward and fingers open. Then twist your open hand back and forth a few times.

✳ Memory tip

It's like tree branches blowing in the wind.

🕐 When to use the sign

You can sign **TREE** while outdoors watching the leaves blow in the wind, while looking at trees through windows at home, or when you see trees in storybooks.

👁 What to look for

Baby might look like he is reaching up and waving or twisting his hand.

flower

With your dominant hand, pinch all your fingers and thumb together. Then touch your fingertips to both sides of your nose.

✳ Memory tip

It's like you're holding a rose petal and smelling it.

🕐 When to use the sign

Flowers are everywhere—in books, on clothing, in vases, and in the garden. Let your baby explore a real flower (with supervision, of course), and teach her the sign for **FLOWER**.

👁 What to look for

It might look like your baby is tapping her nose, chin, or mouth with her whole hand or pointer finger.

bug

Put your thumb on your nose, stick your pointer and middle fingers up toward the sky, and bend those fingers down and up a few times.

✳ **Memory tip**

It's like you're wiggling antennae in front of your nose.

⏰ **When to use the sign**

There are lots of different ASL signs for specific bugs (such as worm, caterpillar, fly, or mosquito), but you can use **BUG** for all insects and multi-legged critters when you're getting started. You'll find the signs for **SPIDER** (page 92) and **BUTTERFLY** (page 92) in this chapter, but feel free to use **BUG** for any and all types of bugs.

👁 **What to look for**

It might look like your baby is opening and closing all his fingers or touching his nose with his hand.

spider

Cross one wrist on top of the other with your palms facing down and wiggle all eight of your fingers.

✳ **Memory tip**

It's like your fingers are the spider's legs.

◉ **When to use the sign**

I love to use this sign when singing "The Itsy Bitsy Spider" (page 97), which you'll find at the end of this chapter.

◉ **What to look for**

Baby might look like she is clasping her hands or just wiggling all of her fingers.

butterfly

With your palms facing your body, cross your hands and hook your thumbs together, then bend both hands repeatedly.

✳ **Memory tip**

It's like your hands are the butterfly's wings flapping.

◉ **When to use the sign**

This sign looks so much like a butterfly that it's easy and fun to do any time you see a butterfly in real life or in a picture. Try using this one at the end of *The Very Hungry Caterpillar* (page 53), which is featured at the end of chapter 3.

◉ **What to look for**

Baby's version of **BUTTERFLY** might look like he's "flying" by flapping both hands, or he might clasp his hands together and open and close his fingers.

out-and-about signs

swing

Start with your nondominant hand in a *U* handshape (page 142) with palm facing down. With your dominant hand, make another *U* handshape with the fingers slightly bent and "sit" them on your opposite fingers, then swing your hands back and forth a few times.

✳ **Memory tip**

It's like your bent fingers are legs and your flat fingers are the seat of the swing.

🕐 **When to use the sign**

If your baby is using an infant swing at home, you can sign **SWING** when you put her in the swing. This is also a great sign to introduce when your baby is big enough to try the baby swings at the playground!

👁 **What to look for**

Baby will likely get the swinging motion of this sign right, but not the handshapes, which are very specific. Look for her clasping her hands together and swinging them back and forth.

I remember trying to get a cute photo of my husband and daughter on Father's Day when she was about 16 months old. We were at a farm and I had the perfect shot set up. Unfortunately, my daughter saw a playground in the distance and wouldn't stop signing **SWING** *until we headed in that direction. The picture is pretty hilarious, but it perfectly captures what her priorities were at the time!*

train

Start with your nondominant hand in a *U* handshape (page 142) with palm facing down. Make another *U* handshape with your dominant hand and slide those fingers back and forth on the opposite two fingers.

✱ **Memory tip**
It's like your bottom fingers are the track and your top fingers are the train.

⏱ **When to use the sign**
Whenever you find the opportunity to talk about trains with baby—when playing with a toy, reading a book, or maybe while watching a real train go by—say and sign **TRAIN** and add a cheerful "choo choo!" to the interaction.

👁 **What to look for**
Baby might rub his pointer fingers together or slide his whole hand over the opposite hand.

bike

Make fists with both hands and rotate them alternately away from your body.

✱ **Memory tip**
It's like your fists are the rotating bike pedals.

⏱ **When to use the sign**
You can sign **BIKE** for a tiny tricycle or a big mountain bike. We used the sign for **BIKE** for a little three-wheeled ride-on toy that didn't even have pedals!

*One time when my daughter was a young toddler, we stopped by the bicycles at the toy store, and she had a great time climbing on the tricycles. Unfortunately, she cried her eyes out when it was time to head home (without a new tricycle). Later that day, she signed **BIKE** for the first time, and we were able to have a nice chat about all the cool bikes we had seen.*

bus

Make *B* handshapes (page 142) with both hands, then put your hands together pinky to thumb, palms facing in opposite directions. Then, move your hands apart and back together.

✳ **Memory tip**

It's like you're showing the length of a long bus or the doors of the bus sliding open and closed.

🕐 **When to use the sign**

Sign **BUS** if you see a bus when you're out and about. You can also use this sign when singing "The Wheels on the Bus" (page 98), which you'll find at the end of this chapter.

👁 **What to look for**

It might look like an awkward clap.

✿ **Similar signs**

BUS is typically fingerspelled in ASL, but this is an acceptable variation and much easier for baby.

airplane

Hold your dominant hand up with your palm facing forward and your thumb, pointer, and pinky fingers extended. Then move your hand upward in a jabbing motion.

✳ **Memory tip**

It's like your hand is an airplane flying up into the sky.

🕐 **When to use the sign**

Sign **AIRPLANE** when you see or hear an airplane overhead or if you have the opportunity to fly with your baby to visit friends or family.

👁 **What to look for**

It might look like your baby is pointing at the sky or reaching up with her whole hand.

✿ **Similar signs**

The handshape for this sign is the same as the one for **I LOVE YOU** (page 131).

SIGNING FUN

Sign and Sing:
"The Itsy Bitsy Spider"

Try swapping out the traditional finger motions for this song with some ASL signs. When I sing this song, I move my **SPIDER** (page 92) as it goes "up the water spout." Remember, you can sign as many or as few of the words in the song as you like.

Key Vocabulary

SPIDER, p. 92   **WATER,** p. 49   **RAIN,** p. 88

SUN, p. 89

The itsy bitsy **SPIDER**

Climbed up the **WATER** spout.

Down came the **RAIN**

And washed the **SPIDER** out.

Out came the **SUN**

And dried up all the **RAIN,**

And the itsy bitsy **SPIDER**

Climbed up the spout again.

Sign and Sing:
"The Wheels on the Bus"

Here's another familiar song that's typically done with hand gestures. Try the following version using ASL signs for a fun spin on the song.

Key Vocabulary

BUS, p. 96   **BABY,** p. 129   **MOM,** p. 125

DAD, p. 126   **I LOVE YOU,** p. 131

The wheels on the **BUS** go round and round,

Round and round, round and round.

The wheels on the **BUS** go round and round

All through the town.

The **BABIES** on the **BUS** cry, "Wah wah wah,

Wah wah wah, wah wah wah."

The **BABIES** on the **BUS** cry, "Wah wah wah,"

All through the town.

The **MOMMIES** on the **BUS** say, "Shhh

shhh shhh,

Shhh shhh shhh, shhh shhh shhh."

The **MOMMIES** on the **BUS** say, "Shhh

shhh shhh,"

All through the town.

The **DADDIES** on the **BUS** say, "**I LOVE YOU,**

I LOVE YOU, I LOVE YOU."

The **DADDIES** on the **BUS** say, "**I LOVE YOU,**"

All through the town.

Sign and Read:
Zoom, Zoom, Baby! by Karen Katz

This cute and colorful lift-the-flap board book includes different types of vehicles and offers lots of opportunities to teach and practice signs like **BUS** (page 96), **AIRPLANE** (page 96), **TRAIN** (page 95) and **CAR** (page 35). You can also practice your animal signs for **RABBIT** (page 107), **MONKEY** (page 115), and more as you find them hiding under the flaps of the book.

Key Vocabulary

BABY, p. 129   **RABBIT,** p. 107   **BUS,** p. 96

MONKEY, p. 115   **AIRPLANE,** p. 96   **BEAR,** p. 115

TRAIN, p. 95   **LION,** p. 116   **CAR,** p. 35

Sign and Read:
I Love You, Sun, I Love You, Moon
by Tomie dePaola

This is a sweet and simple board book with repetitive text that allows us to take a moment to appreciate the beauty of our world. You and your baby will have a chance to practice signing **I LOVE YOU** (page 131) on every page, in addition to practicing nature and animal signs, such as **SUN** (page 89), **MOON** (page 76), **TREE** (page 90), **FLOWER** (page 90), **BUG** (page 91), **STAR** (page 77), **BIRD** (page 106), **FISH** (page 108), **SHEEP** (page 113), and **RABBIT** (page 107).

Key Vocabulary

I LOVE YOU, p. 131   SUN, p. 89   MOON, p. 76

SHEEP, p. 113   TREE, p. 90   BIRD, p. 106

FISH, p. 108   FLOWER, p. 90   RABBIT, p. 107

BUG, p. 91   STAR, p. 77   WATER, p. 49

Sign and Play:
What's Inside?

Babies love to put things in boxes and take them out again! Find a box (an empty tissue box or baby-wipes container work well) and place a toy inside. Shake the box so your baby can hear it rattle around inside. Sign and say, "**WHAT** (page 86) is inside?"

If possible, let your baby pull the item out and then show him the sign for the object. You can use any baby-safe toy that will fit: a small **BALL** (page 33) or rubber **DUCK** (page 111) or any other object you know the sign for. This is also a great way to introduce new signs to your baby.

Key Vocabulary

WHAT, p. 86   **BALL,** p. 33   **DUCK,** p. 111

Sign and Play:
Where Is It?

Babies love peek-a-boo games! It helps them master the concept of object permanence, which is a fancy way of saying that they are learning that something is still there, even when they can't see it. So in addition to being lots of fun, this game is also educational.

To do this activity, take a burp cloth or light blanket and cover a favorite item—maybe a favorite teddy **BEAR**—and then sign and say, "**WHERE** (page 86) is the **BEAR** (page 115)?" Then remove the cloth and say, "There it is! There's the **BEAR**!" as you sign **BEAR** (page 115). Your little one will want to play this over and over, and you can put just about anything you can think of under the blanket. You can even put the blanket over your head or your baby's head and say, "**WHERE** is **BABY** (page 129)?" or "**WHERE** is **MOM** (page 125)?"

Key Vocabulary

WHERE, p. 86   **BEAR,** p. 115   **BABY,** p. 129

MOM, p. 125

7

Animals

WHEN IT COMES to the early talker's vocabulary, a large portion is typically made up of animals and animal sounds—babies are simply fascinated by them. As your baby starts signing, you'll probably find yourself adding more and more animal signs into your daily routines, as you'll be spotting them in toys, books, songs, and just about everywhere!

You already learned how to sign **DOG** (page 31) in chapter 2, but in this chapter, you'll take it further with signs for more pets, like **CAT** (page 105), **BIRD** (page 106), and **FISH** (page 108); farm animals, like **COW** (page 112), **HORSE** (page 112), and **PIG** (page 113); and even zoo animals, like **MONKEY** (page 115), **LION** (page 116), and **GIRAFFE** (page 116)!

And while you won't find every single animal sign here, this chapter will give you more than enough to have fun growing your baby's vocabulary around animals. So go ahead and get started! As you and your baby learn these animal signs, make sure to add some fun animal sound effects. Your little one will love it!

pet signs

cat

Pretend to pinch your cheek with your thumb and pointer finger and pull outward. You can do this sign with one or both hands.

✻ Memory tip

It's like you're showing off your cat whiskers.

🕐 When to use the sign

Sign **CAT** when you see a kitty in real life or in a picture. If you have a cat, your baby might always be looking at it when you're trying to show how to do the sign, so try signing **CAT** while holding the kitty. If your cat doesn't mind, you can even gently sign **CAT** on the kitty's face!

👁 What to look for

It might look like your baby is brushing his face with his fingertips or grabbing at his face.

Kitty *was my older daughter's first spoken word. Don't underestimate your baby's interest in furry family members!*

bird

With your dominant hand, open and close your pointer finger and thumb in front of your mouth.

✳ **Memory tip**

It's like a bird's beak saying "tweet tweet."

🕐 **When to use the sign**

You can sign **BIRD** for any winged creature: bluebird, parakeet, flamingo—you name it!

👁 **What to look for**

Baby might open and close her whole hand near her face or off to the side so it looks more like waving bye-bye.

🧩 **Similar signs**

BIRD and **CHICKEN** are signed the same; however, you can add an optional second step where you "peck" the palm of your opposite hand right after signing **BIRD** in order to specify you mean **CHICKEN**.

rabbit

With your pointer and middle fingers extended, place your hands by the top of your head with your palms facing back, then bend your fingers up and down.

✳ Memory tip

It's like a rabbit's floppy ears.

🕐 When to use the sign

Bunnies are popular characters in children's books, including *Pat the Bunny, Guess How Much I Love You, Knuffle Bunny, The Runaway Bunny,* and more, providing plenty of opportunities to sign **RABBIT**.

👁 What to look for

It might look like your baby is grabbing her hair or scratching her head.

❋ Similar signs

This sign can be done with one or two hands. There is another common version of **RABBIT** where you place your fists end to end in front of your body and "flop" the first two fingers of each hand up and down.

fish

Place your dominant hand flat in front of you, palm facing you with your thumb sticking up. Then move your hand away from you in a swerving motion.

✳ Memory tip

It's like a fish swimming.

🕙 When to use the sign

You can sign **FISH** when looking at fish in an aquarium or a pet store, or if you have a fish toy to play with in the tub. You can also use this sign as an alternative to **CRACKER** (page 46) for fish-shaped snacks.

👁 What to look for

It might look like a flapping hand or the whole arm moving side to side.

🧩 Similar signs

You can also do this sign with two hands by placing your palms together and moving them in a swimming motion.

*Babies often do a simplified version of signs, but on occasion, they can complicate them, as well. My older daughter signed **FISH** by twisting her whole arm backward and to the side and then flapping her hand. She still has a tendency to make things more complicated many years later!*

frog

Place the top of your fist under your chin and pop your pointer and middle fingers out to the side in a *V* handshape (page 142) a few times.

✳ **Memory tip**

It's like a frog's neck bulging out, or frog legs extending as it leaps off a rock.

◑ **When to use the sign**

Sign **FROG** when playing with a frog toy or puppet, or if you see a real frog. Make your best frog noise when using this sign: "Ribbit, ribbit!"

👁 **What to look for**

Baby will likely do the opening and closing movement of this sign with his whole hand, not two fingers.

mouse

With your pointer finger, brush the side of the tip of your nose a few times.

✳ **Memory tip**

It's like a mouse's nose twitching.

◑ **When to use the sign**

Lots of children's books feature mice, such as *Goodnight Moon* and *If You Give a Mouse a Cookie*. Make a game of finding the mouse on each page by asking, "**WHERE** (page 86) is the **MOUSE**? Can you find the **MOUSE**?"

👁 **What to look for**

Baby might poke at his face with his pointer finger or brush his nose with his whole hand.

farm animal signs

duck

Place your pointer and middle fingers together and extend them out in front of your mouth, then open and close your fingers and thumb a few times.

✳ **Memory tip**

It's like a duck's bill opening and closing when it quacks.

🕐 **When to use the sign**

Sign **DUCK** when playing with rubber duckies in the tub or when singing "Five Little Ducks" (page 120), which you'll find at the end of this chapter.

👁 **What to look for**

It might look like your baby is grabbing at her mouth or face, or it might be very similar to how she signs **BIRD** (page 106).

🧩 **Similar signs**

Sometimes **DUCK** is signed with the whole hand instead of just the first two fingers and thumb.

cow

Place your thumb at your temple with your hand in a *Y* handshape (page 142), then twist your hand forward a few times. You can do this sign with one hand or two.

✳ Memory tip

It's like you're showing cow's horns.

◷ When to use the sign

Sign **COW** with a big "moooo!" sound effect whenever you see a cow. You can also sign **COW** when singing "Old MacDonald Had a Farm" (page 118) to baby, which you'll find at the end of this chapter.

◉ What to look for

Baby will likely just touch a pointer finger or thumb to his head and possibly twist it a bit.

horse

Place your thumb at your temple with pointer and middle fingers extended together. Then bend your fingers a few times. You can do this sign with one hand or two.

✳ Memory tip

It's like a horse's ear twitching.

◷ When to use the sign

Sign **HORSE** and say "neigh!" when playing with toy farm animals or reading a book about the farm. You can also sign **HORSE** when singing "Old MacDonald Had a Farm" (page 118) to baby, which you'll find at the end of this chapter.

◉ What to look for

At first, it might look similar to the sign for **RABBIT** (page 107) or **COW** but will start to look more distinctive as your baby's motor skills develop.

sheep

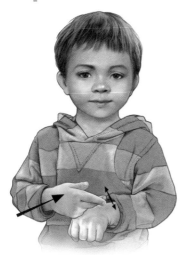

With your dominant hand, open and close your pointer and middle fingers like scissors as you move your hand up the opposite arm.

✳ Memory tip
It's like you're shearing the wool off a sheep.

⊙ When to use the sign
Sign **SHEEP** when playing with farm animal toys, spotting sheep out in nature, or reading a book with a sheep in it, like *Brown Bear, Brown Bear, What Do You See?* (page 119), which is featured at the end of this chapter.

👁 What to look for
It might look like your baby is brushing or rubbing her fingers against her arm.

pig

Place the back of your hand under your chin and bend all of your fingers down together a few times.

✳ Memory tip
It's like food dripping off a pig's chin.

⊙ When to use the sign
Sign **PIG** when playing with farm animal toys or singing "Old MacDonald Had a Farm" (page 118). Be sure to make your best pig noise while doing this sign: "Oink oink!"

👁 What to look for
It might look like your baby is grabbing at his chin or neck.

✿ Similar signs
The sign for **PIG** is similar to the sign for **DIRTY** (page 59).

zoo animal **signs**

monkey

With all of your fingers, scratch both of your sides in an upward motion a few times.

✳ Memory tip

It's just like a silly monkey scratching itself.

🕑 When to use the sign

This sign is lots of fun to do with exaggerated monkey noises and facial expressions. You can also sign **MONKEY** when singing "Five Little Monkeys" (page 138) with your baby. You'll find this song at the end of chapter 8.

👁 What to look for

Baby will surely look like a little monkey when doing this sign!

bear

Cross your arms and scratch your shoulders with your fingers bent.

✳ Memory tip

It's like a bear scratching itself with its big bear claws.

🕑 When to use the sign

Sign **BEAR** when playing with a teddy bear or reading a book like *Brown Bear, Brown Bear, What Do You See?* (page 119), featured at the end of this chapter.

👁 What to look for

Baby might look like she is scratching her chest or belly or giving herself a hug.

My younger daughter did this sign by scratching her belly with one hand.

lion

Curve all your fingers into a "claw" shape and move your hand from the top of your head to the back of your neck.

✳ **Memory tip**

It's like you're showing your big lion's mane.

◉ **When to use the sign**

Sign **LION** when playing with jungle animal toys or reading a fun board book like *Dear Zoo* (page 119), featured at the end of this chapter. Don't forget to roar like a lion when you do this sign!

◉ **What to look for**

It might look like your baby is pulling at his hair.

giraffe

Place your hand in a C handshape (page 142) in front of your neck and then extend your arm up and away from your face.

✳ **Memory tip**

It's like you're showing off the giraffe's long neck.

◉ **When to use the sign**

Sign **GIRAFFE** if your baby has a chewy giraffe toy or when reading *Dear Zoo* (page 119).

◉ **What to look for**

It might look like your baby is reaching up to the sky.

dinosaur

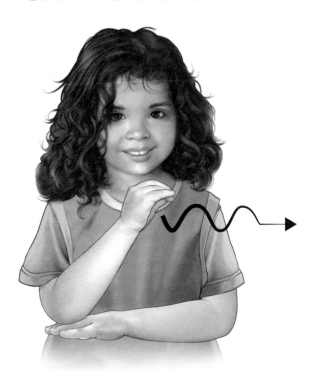

Touch all your fingers to your thumb and move your arm in a heavy up and down motion across the space in front of your body. You can hold your non-dominant arm across your body to support this sign if you like, but it's optional.

✳ **Memory tip**

It's like a big dinosaur lumbering slowly along.

🕐 **When to use the sign**

Unfortunately, dinosaurs are not found at the zoo, but they are so popular in children's toys, clothing, and books that I decided to include the sign here. Sign **DINOSAUR** and roar like a dinosaur when playing with dino toys or reading a book like *Oh My Oh My Oh Dinosaurs!* or *How Do Dinosaurs Go to Sleep?*

SIGNING FUN

Sign and Sing:
"Old MacDonald Had a Farm"

Have fun spicing up this song with some ASL signs. You don't have to stick with just farm animals. Old MacDonald can even have a mouse that squeaks or a lion that roars on his farm! Babies love the animal sounds in this song, so really exaggerate them as you sign and sing.

Key Vocabulary

COW, p. 112   **HORSE,** p. 112   **PIG,** p. 113

SHEEP, p. 113

Old MacDonald had a farm.

E-I-E-I-O.

And on that farm he had a **COW.**

E-I-E-I-O.

With a "moo moo" (sign **COW**) here

And a "moo moo" (sign **COW**) there,

Here a "moo," there a "moo,"

Everywhere a "moo moo."

Old MacDonald had a farm.

E-I-E-I-O.

Repeat with **HORSE** (page 112), **SHEEP** (page 113), **PIG** (page 113), or any other animals you want!

Sign and Read:
Dear Zoo by Rod Campbell

This fun and silly board book features lots of zoo animals, many of which you've learned signs for in this chapter. This is a lift-the-flap book, which baby will enjoy playing with as you read aloud. You'll have a great time going through all the too-big, too-scary, and too-tall animals the zoo sent to be kept as a pet. Fortunately, the zoo finally gets it right at the end!

Key Vocabulary

GIRAFFE, p. 116   **LION,** p. 116   **MONKEY,** p. 115

FROG, p. 109   **DOG,** p. 31

Sign and Read:
Brown Bear, Brown Bear, What Do You See? by Bill Martin and Eric Carle

This classic book is one of my all-time favorites! It features repetitive, rhythmic text that baby will love. You'll be able to sign all the animals in this book based on what you've learned in this chapter. You can also use the sign for **WHAT** (page 86) on each page to emphasize the book's theme of "**WHAT** do you see?" As your baby gets older, this book also works great for introducing colors.

Key Vocabulary

BEAR, p. 115   **WHAT,** p. 86   **BIRD,** p. 106

DUCK, p. 111   **HORSE,** p. 112   **FROG,** p. 109

CAT, p. 105   **DOG,** p. 31   **SHEEP,** p. 113

Sign and Sing:
"Five Little Ducks"

This cute little tune takes a sad turn when mama duck notices that all the little ducklings are gone. Good thing it has a happy ending. This is also a great opportunity to practice family and feelings signs, found in chapter 8. If you'd like, you can also add the ASL signs for the numbers 1 through 5 (page 141).

Key Vocabulary

DUCK, p. 111   **PLAY,** p. 83   **MOM,** p. 125

SAD, p. 133

Five little **DUCKS** went out to **PLAY**

Over the hill and far away.

MAMA DUCK said, "Quack quack quack quack" (sign **DUCK**),

But only four little **DUCKS** came back.

Four little **DUCKS** went out to **PLAY**

Over the hill and far away.

MAMA DUCK said, "Quack quack quack quack" (sign **DUCK**),

But only three little **DUCKS** came back.

Three little **DUCKS** went out to **PLAY**

Over the hill and far away.

MAMA DUCK said, "Quack quack quack quack" (sign **DUCK**),

But only two little **DUCKS** came back.

Two little **DUCKS** went out to **PLAY**

Over the hill and far away.

MAMA DUCK said, "Quack quack quack

quack" (sign **DUCK**),

But only one little **DUCK** came back.

One little **DUCK** went out to **PLAY**

Over the hill and far away.

MAMA DUCK said, "Quack quack quack

quack" (sign **DUCK**),

But none of the five little **DUCKS** came back.

SAD MAMA DUCK went out one day

Over the hill and far away.

SAD MAMA DUCK said, "Quack quack quack

quack" (sign **DUCK**),

And all of the five little **DUCKS** came back.

Sign and Play:
Nice Kitty

If you have a cat or a dog, chances are good that your baby is pretty interested in your four-legged family member. If you don't, you probably have a friend or family member who does! If the pet is good with babies, let your baby pet it. Take this opportunity to teach her the sign for **CAT** (page 105) or **DOG** (page 31) as well as the sign for **GENTLE** (page 134). You can show her what **GENTLE** means by gently signing it on her hand or arm.

Key Vocabulary

CAT, p. 105   **DOG,** p. 31   **GENTLE,** p. 134

8

Family and Feelings

IN THIS CHAPTER, you'll learn signs for family members and important feelings. I think of these as more advanced, "toddler-level" signs, not starter signs, so keep that in mind when introducing them to little ones. While the signs in this chapter are extremely useful, they're probably not the first ones your baby will use.

When introducing signs for family members, you can pair ASL signs with whatever words your family uses for certain family members. For example, if your baby's grandmother goes by Nana, Grammy, Abuela, or Yaya, you can still sign **GRANDMA** (page 127) when talking about her. Remember, you can pair ASL signs with words in any spoken language, as discussed in chapter 1 (see page 10).

Signs for feelings can be really helpful as your baby starts to become more aware of her mood and the feelings of others. Teaching signs for emotions can be challenging because when your baby is having big emotions, it's often not the ideal time to be learning new skills. In this chapter, I share some easy tips to help you teach your baby signs for difficult feelings, like **SAD** (page 133) and **HURT** (page 136).

family signs

mom

With an open hand, tap your thumb on the side of your chin a few times.

mom (alternate)

✳ **Memory tip**

In ASL, all the signs for females (**MOM**, **GRANDMA** [page 127], **SISTER** [page 128]) are done on the lower half of the face, and signs for males (**DAD** [page 126], **GRANDPA** [page 127], **BROTHER** [page 128]) are done on the top half of the face. One way to remember this is that men are generally taller than women.

🕐 **When to use the sign**

Sometimes it's easier for someone other than the mom to teach this sign. Try introducing this sign when someone else is caring for the baby by looking at a picture or signing **MOM** when she walks into the room.

🧩 **Similar signs**

If your family has two moms, or a mom and a stepmom, you can use this alternate version to differentiate the other mom: Touch the thumb of your open hand to the side of your chin and wiggle your fingers a little bit.

I'll be honest, neither of my babies ever signed **MOM**, *but* mama *was one of their first spoken words—yay!*

dad

With an open hand, tap your thumb on the side of your forehead a few times.

dad (alternate)

✳ Memory tip

As mentioned earlier, in ASL, all the signs for males (**DAD**, **GRANDPA** [page 127], **BROTHER** [page 128]) are done on the top half of the face, and signs for females (**MOM** [page 125], **GRANDMA** [page 127], **SISTER** [page 128]), are done on the lower half of the face. One way to remember this is that men are generally taller than women.

🕐 When to use the sign

Just like with **MOM** (page 125), sometimes it's easier for someone other than the dad to teach baby this sign.

🧩 Similar signs

If your family has two dads, or a dad and a stepdad, you can use this alternate version to differentiate the other dad: Touch the thumb of your open hand to the side of your forehead and wiggle your fingers a little bit.

grandma

Start with the thumb of your open hand touching your chin, palm facing out, and bounce your hand away from you two times.

✳ **Memory tip**

It's like you're showing the two generations between baby and grandma.

🕐 **When to use the sign**

Sign **GRANDMA** when grandma comes to visit or when you look at pictures of her.

👁 **What to look for**

Babies often do more than just two bounces with this sign, as they are often excited about seeing grandma!

grandpa

Start with the thumb of your open hand touching your forehead, palm facing out, and bounce it away from you two times.

✳ **Memory tip**

It's like you're showing the two generations between baby and grandpa.

🕐 **When to use the sign**

Sign **GRANDPA** when grandpa is visiting or when you're talking with him on the phone. Using photos is also a great way to introduce and practice signs for family members you might not see every day. See the My Family activity (page 137) in the Signing Fun section at the end of this chapter for more details on how to do this.

sister

Make "L" handshapes (page 142) with both hands. Touch the thumb of your dominant "L" hand at your jaw and bring it down on top of your opposite "L" hand.

✳ **Memory tip**

Like **MOM** (page 125), the sign for **SISTER** starts at the chin because it is a female sign.

🕑 **When to use the sign**

You can pair the sign for **SISTER** with the spoken word *sister* or with the sister's actual name.

👁 **What to look for**

Baby might touch his face with his pointer finger or whole hand, then move it away.

brother

Make "L" handshapes (page 142) with both hands. Touch the thumb of your dominant "L" hand at your forehead and bring it down on top of your opposite "L" hand.

✳ **Memory tip**

Like **DAD** (page 126), the sign for **BROTHER** starts at the forehead because it is a male sign.

🕑 **When to use the sign**

You can pair the sign for **BROTHER** with the spoken word *brother* or the brother's actual name.

👁 **What to look for**

Baby might touch the top of her head with her pointer finger or whole hand, then move it away.

baby

Cradle your arms in front of you and swing them gently from side to side.

✳ **Memory tip**

It's like you're rocking a baby to sleep.

🕐 **When to use the sign**

Sign **BABY** when you see or hear a baby when you are out and about. You can also use this sign for toy babies and dolls.

👁 **What to look for**

It might look like your baby is hugging herself or twisting from side to side.

*This is one of the cutest signs to see a young toddler do! It used to make me laugh when my daughter would see a young child and sign **BABY**, even when the kid was clearly older than my daughter.*

friend

Hook both pointer fingers together in *X* handshapes (page 142), then switch them.

✳ **Memory tip**

It's like two friends giving each other a hug.

🕐 **When to use the sign**

Use the sign for **FRIEND** for playmates and nonfamily members that your baby sees often. It's also a great sign to use when singing "The More We Get Together" (page 38).

👁 **What to look for**

It might look like your baby is touching his pointer fingers together.

feelings signs

i love you

Hold your hand up with your palm facing forward and your thumb, pointer, and pinky fingers extended.

✳ Memory tip

This handshape is a combination of the ASL signs for *I* (page 142), *L* (page 142), and *Y* (page 142), which stands for I-L-Y: **I LOVE YOU**.

🕐 When to use the sign

Sign **I LOVE YOU** anytime you want, especially when parting ways or when saying goodnight.

👁 What to look for

This is a tricky handshape, so babies often do the sign with their whole hand or just the pointer finger extended. I usually add a little shake to this sign—if you do this, too, your baby will probably shake her hand while signing.

This is my number one favorite ASL sign and the only sign that we still use every single day.

happy

With your hand in front of you, palm facing toward you, brush your chest upward a few times.

✳ Memory tip

It's like happy feelings are rising up from your heart.

🕐 When to use the sign

When using signs for emotions, be sure that your facial expression matches the feeling you're communicating. So when you sign **HAPPY**, be sure to smile!

👁 What to look for

It might look like your baby is patting or rubbing his chest or belly.

sad

Start with both hands in front of your face, palms facing your forehead, then move both hands downward to reveal your sad face.

✳ **Memory tip**

It's like your whole face is drooping from the feeling of sadness.

🕐 **When to use the sign**

When your baby is upset, it's generally not a great time to introduce a new sign. Try teaching the sign for **SAD** when you see or hear someone else crying or feeling sad. You can say, "That baby sounds so **SAD**, but I'm sure his mommy will help him feel better!"

👁 **What to look for**

Baby might drag one or both hands over her face.

✱ **Similar signs**

To sign **CRY,** make a sad face and move both pointer fingers down your cheeks like you're showing the tears falling down.

grumpy

Start with your "claw" hand (all fingers bent) in front of your face and slightly unbend and bend your fingers a few times.

✳ Memory tip

It's like you're showing your scrunched-up, grumpy face.

🕐 When to use the sign

Sign **GRUMPY** when your baby wakes up on the wrong side of the crib or is irritable. Say, "You sure are **GRUMPY** today!"

👁 What to look for

Baby might open and close his whole hand in front of his face.

gentle

Make a fist with one hand, and gently stroke the back of your fist with your other hand.

✳ Memory tip

It's like you're gently touching the top of a baby's delicate head.

🕐 When to use the sign

Sign **GENTLE** to help your baby understand when she shouldn't pinch or grab. If she is being too rough with you or a pet, say in a soothing voice, "**GENTLE**. Be sure to use **GENTLE** hands." This is a great sign to do on your baby's hand or arm so she can feel the sensation of a gentle touch.

👁 What to look for

Baby might look like she's rubbing her hands together or brushing her opposite hand or arm.

sorry

Circle your closed fist on your chest.

✳ Memory tip
It's like your heart hurts from hurting someone else.

🕑 When to use the sign
Like other signs for feelings, it's important that your facial expression matches the intention of the sign. Be sure your face conveys concern or regret when you sign **SORRY**.

👁 What to look for
This might look similar to your baby's version of **PLEASE** (page 50), which is a similar motion but done with an open hand.

help

Place your dominant hand in a thumbs-up shape on your opposite palm, then lift them together slightly.

✳ Memory tip
It's like your bottom hand is helping lift your top hand.

🕑 When to use the sign
Ask, "Do you need **HELP**?" when you see her struggling or getting frustrated. In time, baby will let you know she needs **HELP** . . . instead of having a meltdown!

👁 What to look for
Baby might look like she is clasping her hands and bouncing them together.

hurt

Tap your pointer fingers together in front of your body or in front of the body part that hurts.

✳ Memory tip

It's like your fingers are arrows pointing to the part that hurts.

🕐 When to use the sign

If your baby's in pain, it's generally not the best time for him to learn. If he seems upset or uncomfortable, try asking, "Does it **HURT**?" Another great way to teach this sign is to pretend to bump into something (just don't overdo it, because it might really upset him!) and then say, "Ouch, mommy bumped her head. That **HURT**."

👁 What to look for

It might look like your baby is tapping one finger or hand on top of the other or bringing his hands together in a similar way to the sign for **MORE** (page 27).

✿ Similar signs

You can also bring the pointer fingers together in a twisting motion to indicate more intense pain.

*My younger daughter used to drop her dolls and then sign **HURT** with the saddest expression. It was both hilarious and adorable!*

SIGNING FUN

Sign and Read:
"More More More," Said the Baby
by Vera B. Williams

This darling picture book tells the story of three toddlers playing and being loved by family members with kisses and cuddles. It's a great story to practice some family signs as well as the sign for **MORE** (page 27).

Key Vocabulary

MORE, p. 27   **BABY,** p. 129   **DAD,** p. 128

GRANDMA, p. 127   **MOM,** p. 125   **BED,** p. 29

Sign and Play:
My Family

Fill a soft, baby-friendly photo book with pictures of family and friends. Let your baby flip through the photos while you teach him the names of family members as well as the signs. Although it does take a little effort to print the photos and put them in a little album, it will likely become one of his favorite books.

Key Vocabulary

MOM, p. 125   **DAD,** p. 126   **GRANDMA,** p. 127

GRANDPA, p. 127

Sign and Sing:
"Five Little Monkeys"

This song is silly, high energy, and so much fun to sign and sing, especially during playtime! You can really play up the expressions on this one: Make a sad face when the **MONKEY** (page 115) gets **HURT** (page 136), and make a mock-serious face when **MAMA** (sign **MOM**; page 125) scolds the monkeys. Babies will love watching you ham it up. If you're feeling ambitious, you can also use the ASL signs for the numbers 1 through 5, which you can find on page 141.

Key Vocabulary

MONKEY, p. 115

BED, p. 29

HURT, p. 136

MOM, p. 125

Five little **MONKEYS** jumping on the **BED,**

One fell off and bumped (sign **HURT**) his head.

MAMA called the doctor and the doctor said,

"No more **MONKEYS** jumping on the **BED**."

Four little **MONKEYS** jumping on the **BED,**

One fell off and bumped (sign **HURT**) his head.

MAMA called the doctor and the doctor said,

"No more **MONKEYS** jumping on the **BED**."

Three little **MONKEYS** jumping on the **BED,**

One fell off and bumped (sign **HURT**) his head.

MAMA called the doctor and the doctor said,

"No more **MONKEYS** jumping on the **BED**."

Two little **MONKEYS** jumping on the **BED,**

One fell off and bumped (sign **HURT**) his head.

MAMA called the doctor and the doctor said,

"No more **MONKEYS** jumping on the **BED**."

One little **MONKEY** jumping on the **BED,**

He fell off and bumped (sign **HURT**) his head.

MAMA called the doctor and the doctor said,

"Put those **MONKEYS** straight to **BED**."

Sign and Read:
You Are My Sunshine
by Caroline Jayne Church

This is my absolute favorite song to sing to my little ones and many of the families I've worked with over the years. This sweet and simple board book will teach you the lyrics, and you and your baby will enjoy the adorable illustrations as you sing along. Once you've mastered the words, you might find yourself singing this to your baby whenever you have the chance.

Key Vocabulary

SUN, p. 89   **HAPPY,** p. 132   **I LOVE YOU,** p. 131

PLEASE, p. 50

ASL alphabet and numbers

You might be wondering why I'm including the ASL ABCs and 123s in a book called *Baby Sign Language Made Easy*—I mean, isn't this a little advanced? Well, don't worry. You definitely don't need to learn how to fingerspell the whole alphabet or how to count in sign language. But once you start signing with baby, you'll likely find this to be a "handy" (get it?) reference.

I've included the ASL alphabet because many of the signs in this book are based on handshapes from the signed alphabet. For example, the sign for **WATER** (page 49) is made with a *W* handshape, and the sign for **FRIEND** (page 129) is made with two *X* handshapes. You can reference this chart as needed for learning signs based on ASL letters.

You also might want to learn to count for singing and signing songs like "Five Little Monkeys" (page 138) or "Five Little Ducks" (page 120). Counting in ASL is fun because you can count to 10 using just one hand!

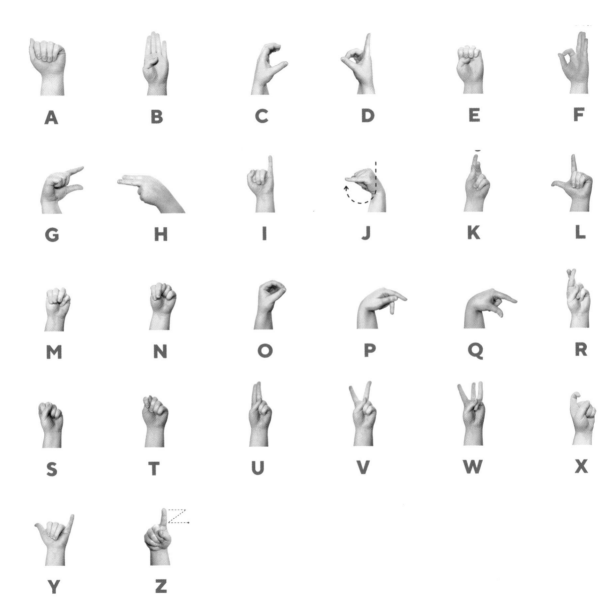

resources

AUTHOR'S WEBSITE

Visit me online for upcoming classes and workshops, as well as helpful resources for baby sign language.

TinySigns.net

ONLINE VIDEO DICTIONARY

You might find it helpful to see the signs you've learned in this book in action. I've created a free video dictionary of all the signs in this book on my Tiny Signs® website, where you can find short videos of me demonstrating each of the signs.

TinySigns.net/book-owner

ASL WEBSITES

If you'd like to learn more about American Sign Language and the Deaf community, the following sites are a great place to start and offer free and paid courses. You can also search online to see if there are any local, in-person ASL classes in your area.

Handspeak.com

Lifeprint.com

SignLanguage101.com

SignItASL.com

SigningOnline.com

StartASL.com

RESEARCH

For findings on the beneficial effects of signs and gestures on infants' language development, see the following.

Baby Signs Too. "The Science behind the Signing." Accessed February 7, 2018. https://www.babysignstoo.com/information/research

Goodwyn, Susan W., Linda P. Acredolo, and Catherine A. Brown. "Impact of Symbolic Gesturing on Early Language Development." *Journal of Verbal and Nonverbal Behavior* 24, no. 2 (2000): 81–103.

Rebelo, Lane. "Using Sign Language with Babies: What the Research Shows." *Tiny Signs*. Accessed February 7, 2018. https://tinysigns.net/baby-sign-language-research/

Two Little Hands Productions. "Research." *Signing Time*. Accessed February 7, 2018. https://www.signingtime.com/resources/research

GREAT PICTURE BOOKS FOR READING AND SIGNING

As you learned throughout this book, story time is one of the best times to sign with baby and to introduce new words and signs. I've compiled a list of my favorite books to read and sign with little ones!

Books highlighted in *Baby Sign Language Made Easy*

Doggies by Sandra Boynton (page 36)

The Very Hungry Caterpillar by Eric Carle (page 53)

Blue Hat, Green Hat by Sandra Boynton (page 67)

The Going to Bed Book by Sandra Boynton (page 78)

Zoom, Zoom, Baby! by Karen Katz (page 99)

I Love You, Sun, I Love You, Moon by Tomie dePaola (page 100)

Dear Zoo by Rod Campbell (page 119)

Brown Bear, Brown Bear, What Do You See? by Bill Martin Jr. and Eric Carle (page 119)

"More More More," Said the Baby by Vera B. Williams (page 137)

You Are My Sunshine by Caroline Jayne Church (page 139)

Other books I love for signing with baby

Baby Happy Baby Sad by Leslie Patricelli

Baby Touch and Feel: Mealtime by DK Publishing

Daddy and Me by Karen Katz

Excuse Me! A Little Book of Manners by Karen Katz

First 100 Words by Roger Priddy

Five Little Ducks by Raffi, Jose Aruego, and Ariane Dewey

Five Little Monkeys Jumping on the Bed by Eileen Christelow

Goodnight Moon by Margaret Wise Brown and Clement Hurd

Itsy Bitsy Spider by Emily Bannister

Let's Get Dressed by Caroline Jayne Church

Pat the Bunny by Dorothy Kunhardt

Peek-a-Moo! by Nina Laden

Splish, Splash, Baby! by Karen Katz

The More We Get Together by Caroline Jayne Church

Tubby by Leslie Patricelli

Twinkle, Twinkle, Little Star by Caroline Jayne Church

Where Is Baby's Mommy? by Karen Katz

index

baby sign language made easy

acknowledgments

Thank you to my editor, Salwa Jabado, for cheering me on and making the writing process a pleasure. Thanks also to the team at Callisto Media for your faith in me and for this opportunity to share my knowledge and experience.

Thanks to my family for your love and encouragement from afar. Heartfelt gratitude to Mom and Bob, Dad and Denise, Scott and Traci, and Diana. Thank you for always asking, "And how are things going with Tiny Signs?"

Thank you to Jen Kettell for being the best friend a girl could wish for, always there to listen with compassion and to share a good laugh.

A special thanks to my smart and curious girlies, Clara and Annie. You are the reason I fell in love with signing. I'm so grateful that our ongoing conversation got started so early on, and I hope it never ends.

Thank you to my husband, André, for your unwavering support and encouragement. You're a keeper.

And, most importantly, thank you to each and every member of the Tiny Signs® community. Whether you took a class or workshop with me here in Massachusetts or learned with me online from around the globe, you are the reason I still love teaching baby sign language after all these years. Answering your questions and sharing in your successes never gets old, and I'm grateful to be a part of your life. Thank you!

about the author

....

LANE REBELO, LCSW, is the founder of Tiny Signs®, an award-winning baby sign language program providing classes, workshops, and professional trainings in the Boston area and online. Lane is a licensed social worker and has worked for many years with families in the Boston area. Lane began studying American Sign Language in 2006 after her first baby was born and was amazed by all she had to say. She lives with her husband and two daughters in MetroWest Boston. You can find her online at TinySigns.net.